CHARACTER TEXT
FOR P. C. T'UNG & D. E. POLLARD
COLLOQUIAL CHINESE

FULL-FORM CHARACTER VERSION

漢語口語
漢字本

PREPARED BY

PING-CHENG T'UNG

ISBN 0 9508572 0 3

Prepared and published by

P.C. T'ung
Senior Lecturer in Chinese (Retired)
School of Oriental and African Studies
University of London

First published 1982
Reprinted 1986, 1989, 1994, 2002, 2004

Printed and bound in Great Britain by
Antony Rowe Ltd, Chippenham, Wiltshire

CONTENTS

BASIC STROKES OF CHINESE CHARACTERS

Basic Strokes	Examples	Some Variants and Combined Strokes		Examples	
丶	文	ノ	′	小	茶
		丶	↘	不	外
一	大	フ	フ	口	五
		フ	フ	同	羽
		フ	フ	刀	力
		フ	フ	又	水
		フ	フ	字	你
		て	て	朵	段
		し	し	凡	亢
		ろ	ろ	及	建
		ろ	ろ	乃	阿
		乙	乙	乙	吃
		て	て	氣	風
丨	中	↓	↓	小	才
		↓	↓	比	衣
		し	し	山	忙
		し	し	也	孔
		ち	ち	馬	巧
丿	人	ノ	ノ	片	月
		′	′	千	位
		ム	ム	系	去
		く	く	女	巡
乀	入	￣	￣	這	走
	法				
乀	家	↘	↘	我	代
		乀	乀	心	必

GENERAL RULES OF STROKE-ORDER OF CHINESE CHARACTERS

1. From top to bottom

   Examples: | 三 | 一 二 三 | 高 | 亠 古 高 |

2. From left to right

   Examples: | 你 | 亻 你 | 啊 | 口 吋 啊 |

3. From outside to inside

   Examples: | 同 | 门 同 | 風 | 几 凬 風 |

4. Left-falling precedes right-falling

   Examples: | 人 | 丿 人 | 又 | フ 又 |

5. Horizontal precedes crossing vertical or other downstroke

   Examples: | 十 | 一 十 | 天 | 二 チ 天 |

6. Box precedes crossing vertical or other downstroke

   Examples: | 中 | 口 中 | 史 | 口 史 史 |

7. Bottom horizontal last

   Examples: | 王 | 二 チ 王 | 正 | 丁 下 正 正 |

8. Inside precedes the sealing stroke

   Examples: | 日 | 冂 日 日 | 因 | 冂 因 因 |

9. Middle precedes the two sides

   Examples: | 小 | 亅 小 小 | 水 | 亅 水 水 |

10. Top left dot first; top right dot last

    Examples: | 為 | 丶 丿 為 為 | 找 | 扌 找 找 |

天	tiān (N) sky; heaven; weather; day (M) for days	也	yě (A) also, too; either
氣	qì [气] (N) air; breath	們	mén * [们] plural suffix for personal pronouns and nouns denoting persons
很	hěn (A) very; quite	忙	máng (SV) busy
好	hǎo (SV) good; well; fine (IE) all right, O.K.	昨	zuó * yesterday 昨天
冷	lěng (冷) (SV) cold	呢	ne (P) particle for follow-up questions
嗎	ma [吗] (P) question particle	早	zǎo (SV) early (IE) good morning!
不	bù (A) not; no, not so	啊	a (P) question and modal particle
熱	rè [热] (SV) hot (of weather); warm	都	dōu [都] (A) all; both; in all cases
今	jīn * at present, now 今天 today	請	qǐng (請) [请] (V) to request; to invite (IE) (will you) please
真	zhēn (眞) (A) truly, really (AT) real, true	坐	zuò (V) to sit; to travel by
我	wǒ (PN) I, me	再	zài (A) again, once more
你	nǐ (PN) you	見	jiàn [见] (V) to see; to meet

您	nín (PN) you (polite form)	她	tā (PN) she, her
他	tā (PN) he, him		

* bound elements —— only occur as constituents of words; do not occur independently

[　] simplified form　　(　) form used only in printing fonts

STROKE—ORDER

天	一 二 于 天	[大]	你	亻 ノ 亻		[人]
氣	气 ノ 一 二 气	[气]	尔	ノ 宀 亇 尓 尔		
	米 、 丷 半 半 米		也	一 也 也		[乙]
(气)			們	亻		[人]
很	彳 ノ ㇠ 彳	[彳]	門	丨 阝 阝 阝 阝 門 門 門		
	艮 コ ㅋ ㅋ 艮 艮 艮		(们)	门 、 亻 门		
好	女 く 女 女	[女]	忙	忄 丨 忄 忄		[心]
	子 ㇇ 了 子		亡	、 二 亡		
冷	冫 、 冫	[冫]	昨	日 丨 冂 日 日		[日]
	令 ノ 人 亼 今 令		乍	ノ 一 亇 乍 乍		
嗎	口 、 口 口	[口]	呢	口 、 口 口		[口]
	馬 一 三 手 馬 馬 馬 馬		尼	㇒ ㇆ 尸 尼 尼		
(吗)	马 ㇆ 马 马		早	、 冂 曰 旦 早		[日]
不	一 ㇀ 不 不	[一]	啊	口 、 口 口		[口]
熱	坴 一 十 土 キ 夫 去 坴			阝 ㇆ ㇆ 阝		
	丸 ノ 九 丸	[火]	可	一 ㅁ 可		
	灬 、 灬 灬 灬 灬		都	者 一 十 土 耂 者 者 者 者		
(热)	扌 一 十 扌			阝 ㇆ ㇆ 阝		[邑]
今	ノ 人 今 今	[人]	請	言 、 二 三 言 言		[言]
真	一 十 广 疒 首 直 真 真	[目]	青	一 二 キ 主 丰 青 青 青		
我	ノ ㇀ 于 手 我 我 我	[戈]	(请)	讠 、 讠		

2

坐 　丶　八　丛　从　丛　半　坐　　[土]　　您　你　亻　亻'　忄'　忻　忺　你　　[心]

再 　一　丆　冂　币　再　再　　　　[冂]　　　　心　丶　心　心　心

見 　丨　冂　月　目　貝　見　　　　[見]　　他　亻　亻一　忚　他　　　　　　　[人]

(见) 　丨　冂　贝　见　　　　　　　　　　　她　乚　夕　女　她　　　　　　　　　[女]

[ ] radical under which this character is classified in the traditional
214 radical system

VOCABULARY

Noun (N)

天氣　tiānqi　weather

Time words (TW)

今天　jīntiān　today

昨天　zuótiān　yesterday

Pronouns (PN)

我　wǒ　I, me

你　nǐ　you

您　nín　you (polite form)

他　tā　he, him

她　tā　she, her

我們　wǒmen　we, us

你們　nǐmen　you (plural)

他們
她們 } tāmen　they, them

Stative verbs (SV)

好　hǎo　good; fine, all right

冷　lěng　cold

熱　rè　hot

忙　máng　busy

早　zǎo　early

Adverbs (A)

很　hěn　very, quite

不　bù　not

真　zhēn　truly, really

也　yě　also, too, either, as well

都　dōu　all, both

Particles (P)

嗎　ma　question particle

呢　ne　particle for follow-up question

啊　a　question and modal particle

Idiomatic expressions (IE)

早!　zǎo　good morning!

請坐　qǐng zuò　please sit down

請　qǐng　(will you) please

你好!　nǐ hǎo　How do you do? How are you?

再見　zàijiàn　goodbye

3

(1) 天氣很好!
　　冷嗎? 不冷.
　　熱嗎? 不熱.

(2) 今天真冷!
　　我很冷,你冷不冷?
　　我也很冷.

(3) 你們不忙嗎?
　　今天不忙,昨天很忙,你們呢?
　　我們今天也不忙.

DIALOGUES

(1) A: 早啊!
　　B: 早!天氣真好.
　　A: 真好,不冷不熱.
　　B: 你們都好嗎?
　　A: 都好,請坐,請坐.
　　B: 好,好!

(2) A: 好啊!
　　B: 你好!
　　A: 天氣真冷!
　　B: 真冷.你們忙不忙?
　　A: 我們都很忙,你們呢?
　　B: 我們也都很忙,再見!
　　A: 再見,再見!

(3) A: 昨天真熱!
　　B: 熱?!
　　A: 您不熱啊?
　　B: 我不熱.
　　A: 真不熱嗎?
　　B: 真不熱!

(1) Contrastive sentences with stative verbs

Pattern: Topic/subject (neg) SV

昨天　　　　　　冷,

今天　　　　　　熱.

1. 冷不好,熱好.　　　　3. 你忙,我忙,他不忙.

2. 他冷,我不冷.

(2) Stative verbs with adverbial modifiers

Pattern: Topic/subject (A) (A) (A) SV

天氣　　　　　　　真 好.

他們　　　都 不 很 忙.

1. 今天很冷.　　　　　4. 天氣很不好.

2. 他們都很冷.　　　　5. 他們不都很忙.

3. 我們也都很冷.

Contrast: ⎰ 不很　天氣不很好. ⎰ 不都　他們不都忙.
　　　　　 ⎱ 很不　天氣很不好. ⎱ 都不　他們都不忙.

(3) Three types of questions

(a) Questions with the interrogative particle ma

Pattern:　　Statement　+　P?

天氣好　　嗎?

1. A: 今天冷嗎?　　　　B: 很冷.

2. A: 他們都好嗎?　　　B: 都好.

5

3. A: 你不熱嗎?　　　　　　B: 我不熱.

4. A: 他們不忙嗎?　　　　　B: 忙! 他們都很忙.

(b) Choice-type questions

Pattern:　Topic/subject　　SV　neg SV?

天氣　　　　好　不　好?

1. A: 今天冷不冷?　　　　　B: 不很冷.

2. A: 你們忙不忙?　　　　　B: 我們都很忙.

3. A: 他熱不熱?　　　　　　B: 他不熱.

(c) Follow-up questions

Pattern:　Topic/subject$_1$ + comment, topic/subject$_2$ + <u>ne</u>?

他們　　　　都好，　你們　　　　呢?

1. A: 你很熱嗎?　　　　　　B: 不熱, 你呢?

2. A: 你們不忙嗎?　　　　　B: 不忙, 你們呢?

3. A: 你冷不冷?　　　　　　B: 很冷, 你呢?

這	zhè, zhèi (這)[这] (SP) this	京	jīng * capital 北京 Peking
是	shì (CLV) to be; to be so (IE) That is so; yes; right	愛	ài [爱] (V) to like; to love (MV) like to; love to
張	zhāng [张] * to extend (M) for paper, table, etc. a common surname	姓	xìng (N) surname (CLV) to be surnamed
華	huá * [华] flowery short for China 中華 Huà a surname	王	wáng (N) king a common surname
同	tóng (SV) same; alike	名	míng * name, given name; fame
志	zhì * ambition; will 同志 comrade	字	zì (N) written character; monosyllabic word
中	zhōng * middle; centre; amidst short for China 中國	英	yīng * [英] flower; brave short for England (U.K.)英國
國	guó [国] (N) country; nation; state * of the state; national	小	xiǎo (SV) small; little; young (of age); low (of voice)

人	rén
	(N) human being, man, person,
	  people
		上	shàng
			(V) to ascend, mount; to go
			   to
			(L) up; top; upper; above

叫	jiào 叫 [叫] (V) to call; to shout; to cause to (CLV) to be called	海	hǎi (N) sea 上海 Shanghai
老	lǎo (SV) old; elderly (A) always; keep .... -ing	姐	jiě * elder sister 姐姐
北	běi (L) north, northern	那	nà, nèi (SP) that in that case

7

先	xiān (A) first; previously	甚	shén　　*　[什] what
生	shēng (V) to give birth to, be born (SV) raw, unripe; unfamiliar	麼	me, mo　*　[么] suffix (in 甚麼 'what'; 這麼 'so, in this manner', etc.)
太	tài (A) too, excessively 太太 Mrs; wife	地	dì (N) earth; ground; land; fields
僑	qiáo　　*　[侨] to reside abroad 華僑 overseas Chinese	方	fāng (SV) square * direction; region a surname
美	měi (SV) beautiful, pretty short for America (USA) 美國	問	wèn　　　[问] (V) to ask; to enquire (a question)
誰	shéi, shuí　　[谁] (QW) who, whom	貴	guì　　　[贵] * your (honorific) (SV) expensive, dear
噢	ō　　　　[噢] (I) Oh!	夫	fū　　　* man; husband
進	jìn (進) *　[进] to enter; to advance	哪	nǎ, něi　* (SP) which
吧	ba (P) particle of suggestion		

' ' variant form

STROKE-ORDER

這　言　丶一亠言言　　[这] 是　日　丨冂日日　　[日]
辶　丶氵辶　　　　　　　　 疋　一丁下疋疋
(这) 文　丶亠方文　　　　　　 張　弓　丨引弓　　　　[弓]
辶　丶氵辶　　　　　　　　 長　一丆匚厍臣長長長

8

〔张〕 弓

长　丿一 长 长

華　丶 十 艹 艹 苎 苎 莖 蓹 莗 華

（华）化　亻 亻 化　　　　[艹]

十　一 十

同　丨 冂 冂 同　　　　[口]

志　士 一 十 士　　　　[心]
心　丶 心 心 心

中　丶 口 口 中　　　　[丨]

國　丨 冂 冂 同 同 國 國 國 國 [口]
（国）丨 冂 冂 冃 囯 国 国 国

人　丿 人　　　　[人]

叫　口 叨 叫　　　　[口]

老　一 十 土 耂 耂 老　　[老]

北　丨 十 キ 北 北　　　[匕]

京　丶 一 古 亨 京 京　　[亠]

愛　爫 丶 爫 爫 爫 愛　　[心]
夂　丿 ク 夂 （爱）孚 旁 爱

姓　女 女 妒 妒 姓 姓　　[女]

王　一 二 干 王　　　　[王]

名　丿 ク 夕 名　　　　[口]

字　宀 丶 宀 宀　　　　[子]
子　了 了 子

英　艹 丶 十 艹 艹　　　[艹]
央　丶 口 史 央 央

（英）艹 一 十 艹

小　亅 小 小　　　　[小]

上　丨 十 上　　　　[一]

海　氵 丶 冫 氵　　　　[水]

每　丿 亠 乞 每 每 每 每

姐　女 如 妲 妲 姐　　　[女]

那　刵 刁 刁 刌 刵　　　[邑]
阝 阝 了 阝

先　丿 一 屮 生 屮 先　　[儿]

生　丿 一 亡 牛 生　　　[生]

太　一 ナ 大 太　　　　[大]

僑　亻　　　　[人]
喬　丿 二 千 夭 呑 吞 喬 喬

（侨）亻 仁 伙 侨 侨

美　丶 丷 丷 兰 关 美 美　[羊]

誰　言 訁 訁 訌 訛 誰 誰　[言]
（谁）讠 丶 讠

噢　口　　　　[口]
亻 亻 门 门 冎 冎 用 開 閉 閉 奥

進　亻 亻 仹 佳 佳 進　　[辵]
（进）井 一 二 于 井

吧　口　　　　[口]
巴　丁 丌 口 巴

甚　一 十 廿 甘 甘 其 其 甚　[廿]

（什）亻 亻 什

麼　麻 丶 广 广 斤 庐 庐 麻 [麻]
么　丿 么 么 （么）

地　一 十 土 圤 地 地　　[土]

方　丶 一 亠 方　　　　[方]

問　丨 尸 尸 尸 尸 門 門 門 問 [口]
（问）丶 讠 门 问

貴　口 中 虫 虫 贵 眚 贵 貴 [貝]
（贵）口 中 虫 贵 贵 贵

夫　一 二 龶 夫　　　　[大]

哪　口 叮 叮 叨 哪 哪　　[口]

9

VOCABULARY

Specifiers (SP)

這 zhè, zhèi   this

那 nà, nèi   that

Nouns

同志 tóngzhì   comrade

人 rén   person

愛人 àiren   spouse

姓 xìng   surname

名字 míngzi   given name; full name

小姐 xiáojie   young lady; Miss

先生 xiānsheng   gentleman; Mr; husband

太太 tàitai   lady; Mrs; wife

華僑 huáqiáo   overseas Chinese

地方 dìfang   place

夫人 fūren   madam; Mrs

Classificatory verbs (CLV)

是 shì   to be; to be so

叫 jiào   call; be called

姓 xìng   be surnamed

Stative verbs

老 lǎo   old

小 xiǎo   young; small

Place words (PW)

中國 Zhōngguó   China

北京 Běijīng   Peking

上海 Shànghǎi   Shanghai

英國 Yīngguó   England, GB, UK

美國 Měiguó   America (USA)

Question words (QW)

誰 shéi, shuí   who(m)

甚麼 shénme   what

哪 nǎ, něi   which

Particle

吧 ba   particle of suggestion

Interjection (I)

噢 ō/ò   oh (I see)

Idiomatic expressions

請進 qǐng jìn   come in ('please enter')

請問 qǐng wèn   excuse me, (followed by a question)

貴姓 guì xìng   what is your name? (polite:'honourable surname')

Surnames

張 Zhāng

王 Wáng

10

(1)　這是張華同志.
　　　他是中國人.
　　　我們都叫他老張.
　　　老張是北京人.
　　　他愛人姓王,名字叫英英.
　　　我們都叫她小王.
　　　小王是上海人.

(2)　這是張小姐.
　　　那是王先生,王太太.
　　　他們都是華僑.
　　　他們是哪國華僑?
　　　張小姐是英國華僑.
　　　王先生,王太太是美國華僑.

DIALOGUES

(1)　張：誰啊?
　　　王：我啊!
　　　張：你是誰?
　　　王：我是老王啊.
　　　張：噢!老王,是你啊,請進,請進!
　　　王：你們都好吧?
　　　張：都好,請坐,請坐!
　　　王：天氣真好!
　　　張：真好,不冷不熱!

(2)　A：同志,你姓甚麼?
　　　B：我姓張.
　　　A：叫甚麼名字?
　　　B：張華.
　　　A：張同志甚麼地方人?
　　　B：我北京人.
　　　A：你愛人也是北京人嗎?
　　　B：不是,她是上海人.

(3)　A：請問,您貴姓?
　　　B：我姓王,我叫王同.您是張同志吧?
　　　A：是,我叫張華.王先生,您是哪國人?

11

B： 我是英國人，這是我太太，她是美國人。

A： 王夫人，您好！

C： 您好！張同志是不是上海人？

A： 不是，我是北京人，我愛人是上海人。

(4)　A： 你是王同志吧？

B： 不是，我姓張。

A： 噢，張同志，你是不是叫張英？

B： 不是，我名字叫張京。

A： 他們都叫你小張吧？

B： 不，他們都叫我老張。

A： 張同志是北京人吧？

B： 不是，我是上海人。

A： 你愛人也是上海人吧？

B： 甚麼？！我愛人？！誰是我愛人？！

SPEECH PATTERNS

(1) Sentences with classificatory verbs

Pattern:　Nominal expression　(neg)　CLV　Nominal expression

他　　　　　(不)　是　　英國人　．

1.　他姓王，我不姓王。

2.　他是英國人，你也是英國人嗎？

3.　他姓王，名字叫華中。

4.　他是王華中，王先生。

12

(2) Sentences with object and complement

Pattern:　S　　(neg)　V　O　　Complement
　　　　　他們　　(不)　叫　他　　小　王　。

1.　我們不叫他小王,我們叫他老王。
2.　你們不叫她張小姐嗎? 不叫,我們叫她張同志。
3.　他是北京人,我們都叫他'老北京'。
4.　老王真好,我們都叫他好好先生。

(3) Sentences with question words

Pattern:　　他是誰? 這是甚麼? 他是哪國人?

1.　他姓甚麼? 他姓王。
2.　他叫甚麼名字? 他叫王華中。
3.　他甚麼地方人? 他上海人。
4.　張小姐是哪國人? 她是美國人。
5.　她叫張甚麼? 她叫張美。
6.　她愛人叫王甚麼中? 他叫王華中。
7.　你們叫他甚麼? 我們叫他老王。

(4) Sentences with the particle 'ba'

Pattern:　　　　Statement　　+　　ba?
　　　　　　您是中國人　　　吧　?

1.　你們都好吧?　　都好,你們呢?
2.　今天不忙吧?　　今天不忙,昨天很忙。
3.　他不是美國人吧?　　不是,他是英國人。
4.　他們都是華僑吧?　　是,他們都是英國華僑。

喝	hē (V) to drink	吃	chī (V) to eat; to take (medi- cine)
咖	kā　　　* 咖啡　coffee	外	wài　　　* outside, outer, outward; external; foreign
啡	fēi　　　* 咖啡　coffee	菜	cài　　　[菜] (N) vegetable; dish (of food); cuisine
只	zhǐ (A) only, merely	學	xué　　　[学] (V) to study, to learn; to imitate
茶	chá　　　[茶] (N) tea	話	huà　　　[话] (N) spoken words, speech
看	kàn (V) to look, look at; to see; to visit; to **read**; to think (have a view)	法	fǎ　　　* method; law Fǎ (or Fà) short for France 法國
電	diàn　　　[电] (N) electricity * electric	德	dé　　　* virtue; morality short for Germany 德國
視	shì (視)　[视] (LC) to look at; to regard 　　　as; to inspect 電視 television	會	huì　　　[会] (MV) can (know how to) (V) to meet (N) meeting; association
文	wén　　　* writing; language; culture (SV) literary; elegant	說	shuō (說)　[说] (V) to speak, to say; to 　　　explain; to scold
書	shū　　　[书] (N) book (LC) to write; letter; 　　　document	常	cháng (A) often; usually; 　　　habitually (AT) ordinary
喜	xǐ　　　* to rejoice; joy	飯	fàn (飯)　[饭] (N) cooked rice; meal; food
歡	huān　　*[欢] joyful, merry	應	yīng　　*　[应] ought to; should; must

該	gāi [该] (MV) ought to; should (V) to owe; be sb.'s turn to do sth.	友	yǒu * friend; friendly 朋友 friend
一	yī (NU) one (AT) whole; all; throughout	晚	wǎn (SV) late 晚上 evening
點	diǎn [点] (N) dot; point; speck (V) to dot; to order (a dish)	做	zuò (V) to do; to make (CLV) to be; to act as
兒	ér * [儿] child; non-syllabic diminu- tive suffix	水	shuǐ (N) water * liquid
想	xiǎng (V) to think, to think (that) (MV) want to, plan to, feel like	謝	xiè [谢] (V) to thank a surname
朋	péng * friend, companion	酒	jiǔ (N) wine, spirits, strong drink

STROKE-ORDER

喝　口　　　　　　　　　　　[口]　　視　礻　ヽ ラ 礻 礻　　　　[見]
　　日　ヽ 冂 日 日　　　　　　　　　　見
　　匈　ノ 勹 勹 匃 匈　　　　　　　(视)　礻 礻 視

咖　口 叩 叻 咖　　　　　　　[口]　　文　ヽ 一 ナ 文　　　　　　[文]
啡　口 미 미 미 미 咿 啡 啡　[口]　　書　フ ヲ ヨ ヨ 聿 書 書　[曰]
只　口 只 只　　　　　　　　[口]　　(书)　一 ヲ 书 书
茶　卄 艾 芐 茶 茶 茶 (茶)　[艸]　　喜　一 十 士 吉 吉 壴 喜 喜　[口]
看　手　ノ 三 手　　　　　　[目]　　歡　藋 卄 苗 苗 萑 藋 藋　[欠]
　　目　丨 冂 目 目 目　　　　　　　　　欠　ノ 一 欠
電　雨　一 一 一 丙 雷 雷　[雨]　　(欢)　フ ヌ 欢
　　电　ヽ 冂 曰 日 电　　　　　　　　吃　口 叮 吽 吃　　　　　　[口]
　　(电)　ヽ 冂 日 日 电　　　　　　外　ノ ク タ 列 外　　　　　[夕]

15

菜　艹　　　　　　　　　　　　　　　［艸］　　該　言　　　　　　　　　　　　　［言］
　　采　丶⺈⺥白平采　　　　　　　　　　　　亥　丶一亠亥亥
學　與　丿x方支𣃔段闁與　　　　　　　(该)　讠该
　　一　丶一　　　　　　　　　　　　　［子］　點　黑　丶⼞四四黒里黑　［黑］
　　子　　　　　　　　　　　　　　　　　　　占　丨卜占
(学)　丶丷⺌⺍⺌学学学　　　　　　　　　　(点)　卜占点
話　言言訁訂計話　　　　　　　　　　［言］　兒　丿人⺅⺅竹臼夕兒　　　［儿］
(话)　丶讠话　　　　　　　　　　　　　　　　(儿)　丿儿
法　氵氵汁沣法法　　　　　　　　　　［水氵］　想　木　一十才木　　　　　　［心］
德　彳　丿⺁彳　　　　　　　　　　　［彳］　　　目
　　悳　一十古古古直悳　　　　　　　　　　　心
會　人亼今命命命侖會　　　　　　　　［曰］　朋　丿月月月朋朋朋　　　　　［月］
(会)　人亼仝会会　　　　　　　　　　　　　友　一ナ方友　　　　　　　　　［又］
說　訁訜訰説　　　　　　　　　　　　［言］　晚　日　　　　　　　　　　　　　［日］
(说)　讠说　　　　　　　　　　　　　　　　免　丿⺈⺈⼞凸免免
常　⺌　丶丷⺌⺍⺌　　　　　　　　　［巾］　做　亻仁仕什佔佔做做　　　　　［亻］
　　口　　　　　　　　　　　　　　　　　　水　丨⺈水水　　　　　　　　　［水］
　　巾　丶口巾　　　　　　　　　　　　　　謝　言　　　　　　　　　　　　　［言］
飯　食　丿人⺈今今今食食　　　　　　　　　身　丿⺅⺅白月月身
　　反　丿⺁厂反　　　　　　　　　　［食食］　寸　一寸
(饭)　饣丿⺈饣　　　　　　　　　　　　　　(谢)　讠谢谢
應　丶亠广广府雁應　　　　　　　　　［心］　酒　氵　　　　　　　　　　　　［酉］
(应)　丶亠广广应应应　　　　　　　　　　　酉　一厂丙丙丙两酉

16

VOCABULARY

Verbs (V)

愛 ài love

喝 hē drink

看 kàn look at; read

   看書 kàn-shū (V-O) read

喜歡 xǐhuan like

吃 chī eat

   吃飯 chī-fàn (V-O) eat

學 xué learn

會 huì know (languages)

說 shuō say; speak

   說話 shuō-huà (V-O) speak

想 xiǎng think

做 zuò do; make

謝謝 xièxie thank

Modal verbs (MV)

愛 ài love to, like to, be keen on

喜歡 xǐhuan like to

會 huì can; know how to; have capacity for

應該 yīnggāi should, ought to

想 xiǎng want to; plan to; feel like

Nouns

咖啡 kāfēi coffee

茶 chá tea

電視 diànshì television

中文 Zhōngwén Chinese language

文 wén writing, written word; language

書 shū book

菜 cài vegetables; food (not cereals); dish of food

話 huà speech, spoken words

英文 Yīngwén English language

法文 Fǎwén French language

德文 Déwén German language

飯 fàn cooked rice or other cereals; meal

(一)點兒 (yì)diǎnr a little, some

朋友 péngyou friend

水 shuǐ water

酒 jiǔ wine, spirits, strong drink

Adverbs

只 zhǐ only

常(常) cháng(cháng) often, habitually

Place words

外國 wàiguó abroad, foreign parts

法國 Fǎguó France

德國 Déguó Germany

Time word

晚上 wǎnshang evening

Idiomatic expression

謝謝 xièxie thank you

PRESENTATION

　　王先生、王太太是英國華僑。王先生愛喝咖啡,王太太不愛喝咖啡,她只愛喝中國茶。王先生愛看電視,王太太不愛看電視,她只愛看中文書。王先生喜歡吃外國菜,王太太不喜歡吃外國菜,她只喜歡吃中國菜。王先生很喜歡學外國話,英文、法文、德文,他都會。王太太不喜歡學外國話,她只會說中國話。她常說:"外國人吃外國飯,應該說外國話;中國人吃中國飯,應該說中國話!"

DIALOGUE

王: 今天咖啡真好,你也喝一點兒吧!

太: 不喝,我這茶很好。

王: 看不看電視?

太: 不看,我想看點兒書。

王: 是英文書嗎?

太: 不是,是中文書。誰看英文書?!

王: 朋友都說你應該學點兒英文。

太: 我不學!'外國人說外國話,中國人說中國話'不是很好嗎?!

王: 好,好,不學,不學。晚上做點兒法國菜好不好?

太: 誰做啊?我不會做法國菜,你想吃,你做吧!

18

(1)

A: 老張,喝不喝茶?

B: 不喝。

A: 喝點兒咖啡吧?

B: 不喝。

A: 水呢?

B: 謝謝你,也不喝。

A: 茶、咖啡、水,都不喝,你想喝甚麼?

B: 我想喝點兒酒。

(2)

A: 請坐,請坐!今天真冷,喝點兒茶吧!

B: 謝謝,謝謝,這茶真好,是中國茶吧?

A: 是,您常喝中國茶嗎?

B: 常喝,我很喜歡喝中國茶。

A: 您也喜歡吃中國菜嗎?

B: 很喜歡。

A: 會做不會?

B: 只會吃,不會做!

SPEECH PATTERNS

(1) Sentences with action verbs

Pattern: S (A) V O (P)
　　　　　他　　看中文書

1. 你們喝甚麼?　　他喝咖啡,我喝茶。
2. 晚上誰做飯?　　我做,你吃不吃?
3. 你不看電視嗎?　　不看,我看書。
4. 他喝法國酒,你喝哪國酒?　　我喝德國酒。
5. 他愛人常常做中國菜嗎?　　不常做。

(2) <u>Sentences with modal verbs</u>

Pattern:　　S　(A)　MV　V　O　(P)

　　　　　　　他　　　會　說　中國話.

1. 你愛喝茶嗎?　　很愛喝.
2. 誰想學中文?　　他想學,我也想學.
3. 我很喜歡吃北京菜,你呢?　　我只喜歡吃上海菜.
4. 你們都會說外國話嗎?　　不都會.
5. 我們都應該學做飯嗎?　　都應該.

(3) <u>Choice-type questions with objects (or complements)</u>

Pattern:　　S　(MV)　V　O　bu　(MV)　V ?

　　　　　　　他　　　看電視　不　　看?(=他看不看電視?)

1. 他是北京人不是?　　不是,他是上海人.
2. 他們喝酒不喝?　　不喝,他們都不會喝.
3. 你會做中國菜不會?　　不會(做).
4. 他想學中文不想?　　很想(學).
5. 你喜歡看中文書不喜歡?　　很不喜歡(看).

(4) <u>Sentences with co-ordinated subjects/topics in succession</u>

Pattern:　你,我,他,都不是中國人.

1. 茶,咖啡,都不很熱.
2. 法文、德文,他都會說.

20

3. 中國菜、法國菜,他都不愛吃.
4. 喝法國酒、吃中國菜,誰不喜歡?
5. 他中文書、英文書,都想看.

(5) Co-ordinate clauses with different objects to the same verb

Pattern: S   V O_1, $\underline{y\check{e}}$ V O_2
我 喝 酒, 也 喝 咖啡.

1. 他會說英文,也會說法文.
2. 我想學中文,也想學德文.
3. 他喜歡北京,也喜歡上海.
4. 她常做法國菜,也常做中國菜.
5. 我應該謝謝你,也應該謝謝他.

(6) The use of '(yì)diǎnr'

1. 天氣真熱,我想喝點兒水.
2. 朋友都說你應該學點兒法文.
3. 你會說中國話嗎? 　 會(說)一點兒.
4. 請你做點兒上海菜,好不好?
5. 今天晚上你想做甚麼? 　 我想看點兒書.

21

有	yǒu (V) to have; to exist; there is/are	年	nián (N/M) year
位	wèi (M) polite classifier for persons	三	sān (NU) three
普	pǔ (普) * universal; general	十	shí (NU) ten
通	tōng [通] (V) to go through; lead to; have clear passage (SV) passable; logical	二	èr (NU) two
能	néng (MV) can, be capable of	歲	suì [岁] (M) year of age
沒	méi [没] (A) not (negator for yǒu 有) * without; -less; un-...-ed	四	sì (NU) four
師	shī [师] (LC) teacher 老師 teacher	個	gè [个] (M) general classifier
兩	liǎng [两] (NU) two (used with measures) a couple of (M) 1/10 of a catty (=50g)	女	nǚ * woman; female; daughter
本	běn (M) volume; copy * root; this, the present	子	zǐ * son; child noun suffix
典	diǎn * record; code; rites; classic 字典 dictionary	因	yīn * cause; because; reason for
漢	hàn * [汉] Han people (Chinese majority race); Han Dynasty; man	為	wèi (爲) * [为] for; on account of; for the sake of
就	jiù (A) then; only; right away; just	孩	hái * child 孩子

Char	Reading & meaning	Char	Reading & meaning
所	suǒ　　　* 'that which'; place; office; institute (M) for buildings	幾	jǐ　　　[几] (QW) how many ? (small numbers)
以	yǐ　　　* (LC) to take; to use; by; with; by means of 所以 therefore	大	dà (SV) big, large; eldest (child)
總	zǒng (總)*　　[总] general; in every case; all the time; always	妹	mèi　　　* younger sister 妹妹
累	lèi (SV) tired, weary; fatiguing	知	zhī　　　* to know
要	yào (V) to want; to ask for (MV) want to; be about to; will	道	dào　　*　[道] way; reason; principle; to say; Taoism
多	duō (SV) many, much (A) how (adverb of degree)	媽	mā　　　[妈] (N) mum, mother
可	kě　　　* may, be permitted (A) indeed, certainly	少	shǎo (SV) few, little (V) to lack; to be in want of
父	fù　　　* father	五	wǔ (NU) five
母	mǔ　　　* mother 父母 parents	六	liù (NU) six
定	dìng (V) to fix; to decide on (AT) fixed; settled 一定 definitely, certainly	七	qī (NU) seven
孫	sūn　　*　[孙] grandson 孫子 孫女 granddaughter	八	bā (NU) eight
杯	bēi * cup, glass (M) cup of, glass of	九	jiǔ (NU) nine
共	gòng　　　* together; to share together 一共 altogether; in all		

Character	Stroke order	Radical
有	一 ナ 冇 有 有 有	[月]
位	亻 亻 位 位 位 位	[人]
普	丷 ㇒ ㇒ 並 並 並 並 普	[日]
通	𠃌 マ ㇇ 丹 甬 甬 通 (通)	[辵]
能	㇜ ㇜ 牟 育 育 育 能 能 能	[肉月]
沒	氵 氵 沙 汐 沒 沒 (没)	[水]
師	𠂤 ㇒ ㇒ 𠂤 𠂤 𠂤	[巾]
帀	一 ㇒ 币 币 (师) ㇒ 丨 师	
兩	一 ㇠ ㇇ 雨 雨 兩 兩 兩	[入]
(两)	一 ㇇ 丙 丙 两 两	
本	一 十 才 木 本	[木]
典	丶 口 曰 曲 曲 典 典	[八]
漢 莫	一 十 廿 廿 苫 莒 莫 莫	[水]
(汉)	氵 汀 汉	
就	亠 古 京 京 京 就 就	[尤]
年	丿 ㇒ ㇠ ㇏ 上 年	[干]
三	一 二 三	[一]
十	一 十	[十]
二	一 二	[二]
歲 止	止 ㇒ 丨 ㇠ 止 止	[止]
戌	一 厂 厂 斤 斤 戌 戌 戌	
(岁)	㇒ 山 山 岁 岁 岁	
四	丨 ㇂ 四 四 四	[口]
個	亻 亻 们 们 们 個 個	[人]
(个)	人 个	
因	丨 冂 冂 因 因 因	[口]
為	丶 ㇒ 少 为 为 為 為	[爪]
(为)	丶 ㇒ 为 为	
孩	㇇ 了 孑 孑 孖 孖 孩 孩 孩	[子]

Character	Stroke order	Radical
所	㇒ 𠂆 𠂆 户 户 所 所 所	[戶]
以	丶 丷 以 以 以	[人]
總	糸 ㇜ ㇜ 幺 糸 糸 糸	[糸]
悤	亻 忄 忉 切 匆 匆 悤	
(总)	丶 丷 总 总	
累	丶 冂 曰 田 田	[糸]
糸	㇜ ㇜ 幺 糸 糸 糸	
要	一 厂 厂 両 両 西 要 要 要	[西]
多	㇒ 夕 夕 多 多 多	[夕]
可	一 口 可	[口]
父	㇒ 八 父 父	[父]
母	㇜ 口 母 母 母	[母]
定	丶 丷 宀 宀 宇 定 定	[宀]
孫	子 孑 孖 孫 孫 孫 孫	[子]
(孙)	子 孖 孖 孙	
杯	一 十 才 木 杧 杮 杯 杯	[木]
共	一 十 廿 共 共 共	[八]
幾	幺 糸 絲 絲 幾 幾 幾 幾	[玄]
(几)	丿 几	
大	一 ナ 大	[大]
妹	女 ㄑ 妅 妋 姝 妹	[女]
知	㇒ 二 矢 矢 知	[矢]
道	丷 丷 首 首 首 道 (道)	[辵]
媽	女 女 妈 媽 媽	[女]
(妈)	女 妈 妈 妈	
五	一 丁 五 五	[二]
六	丶 丷 六 六	[八]
七	一 七 [一]　八 ㇒ 八	[八]
九	丿 九	[乙]

24

<u>VOCABULARY</u>

Numbers (NU)

一 yī one (2nd tone before 4th, 4th tone before 1, 2, 3)

二 èr two

兩 liǎng two (used with measures), a couple of

三 sān three

四 sì four

五 wǔ five

六 liù six

七 qī seven }
八 bā eight } optionally 2nd tone before 4th tone

九 jiǔ nine

十 shí ten

Measures (M)

位 wèi polite classifier for persons

本 běn classifier for books

年 nián year

歲 suì year of age

個 gè general classifier

杯 bēi cup of, glass of

天 tiān day

Nouns

普通話 pǔtōnghuà common language, lingua franca, Mandarin

老師 lǎoshī teacher

字典 zìdiǎn dictionary

漢 Hàn Han dynasty; majority people in China; Chinese(in certain combinations)

女兒 nǚ'ér daughter

兒子 érzi son

孩子 háizi child

父母 fùmǔ father and mother

孫子 sūnzi grandson

妹妹 mèimei younger sister

媽 mā mum, mother (familiar)

Stative verbs

普通 pǔtōng common, ordinary

累 lèi tired, weary; fatiguing

多 duō many, much

大 dà big, large; eldest (child)

少 shǎo few, little

Verbs

有 yǒu have; exist; there is/are

生 shēng give birth to, produce; be born

想要 xiǎngyào desire

要 yào want; ask for

知道 zhīdao know

Movable adverbs (MA)

因為 yīnwei because

所以 suǒyǐ therefore

為甚麼 wèishenme why (because of what?)

可是 kěshi but

一共 yígòng altogether

Modal verbs

能 néng can, be capable of

要 yào want to; be about to, will

Adverbs

沒 méi negator for 'yǒu' 有

就(是) jiù(shi) be precisely, exactly, indeed

總(是) zǒng(shi) always

這麼 zhème so (this-wise); also pron. 'zème'

那麼 nàme so (that-wise); also pron. 'nème'

一定 yídìng definitely, certainly

太 tài too, excessively

Time word

今年 jīnnián this year

Question words

幾 jǐ how many (small numbers)

多少 duōshao how many

Measures

個: 一個人；兩個朋友；三個地方；四個孩子；五個甚麼?

位: 六位朋友；七位老師；八位華僑；九位同志；幾位小姐?

本: 九本書；十本字典

杯: 兩杯茶；一杯咖啡；三杯酒

歲: 七十歲

年: 二十五年

天: 十四天

26

PRESENTATION

　　我有一位朋友姓王,是上海人,我們都叫他小王.小王會説上海話,也會説普通話;能看中文書,也能看英文書.他學英文沒有老師,只有兩本字典:一本英漢字典,一本漢英字典.他説這兩本字典就是兩位老師.小王今年三十二歲,有四個女兒,沒有兒子.因為這四個孩子都很小,所以他總是很忙,很累.有一位朋友問他為甚麽要生這麽多孩子,是不是因為想要個兒子?小王説:"我不想要兒子,可是我父母一定要個孫子!"

DIALOGUE

A: 真累,真累!

B: 喝杯茶吧.是不是因為天氣太熱?

A: 不是,是因為孩子太多.

B: 你一共有幾個?

A: 四個,都是女兒.

B: 為甚麽要生那麽多?是不是想要個兒子?

A: 我們不想要兒子,可是我父母一定要個孫子!

B: 這個是你大女兒吧?今年幾歲?

C: 我五歲.

B: 你有幾個妹妹?

C: 不知道.

B: 不知道?! 為甚麽?

C: 我媽常常生妹妹,我也不知道她一共要生幾個.

(1)

A: 一共有多少? 很多吧?

B: 一、二、三、四、五、六、七、....

A: 有沒有四十個?

B: 不知道. 八、九、十、十一、十二......

A: 我們一個人有幾個?

B: 你能不能不說話? 十三、十四、十五...... 一共二十七個.

A: 甚麼?! 只有二十七個?! 這麼少?!

B: 我們九個人, 三九、二十七, 一個人三個, 不多也不少!

(2)

A: 你知道那兩個人是誰嗎?

B: 哪兩個?

A: 那兩個, 你看! 就是那兩個外國人.

B: 噢, 他們啊, 一位是我們法文老師, 一位是我們德文老師.

A: 他們兩位都會說中國話嗎?

B: 都會. 他們總是說中國話, 很少說法文, 也很少說德文.

A: 為甚麼?

B: 因為法文老師不會說德文, 德文老師也不會說法文.

SPEECH PATTERNS

(1) Quantification of nouns

Pattern: Number Measure Noun

三　　　個　　　人

28

1. 他有兩個中國朋友,都姓王.
2. 你要幾本字典?　　三本.
3. 他們有幾個孩子?　　兩個,一個七歲,一個九歲.
4. 他們要多少本?　　六十本.
5. 我想喝杯茶.　　請坐,請坐!
6. 你們有多少人?　　四十八個.
7. 一共多少天?　　十五天.

(2) Specification of nouns

Patterns:　SP　NU　M　N
　　a.　這　　　　　茶
　　b.　這　(一)　杯　茶
　　c.　那　三　杯　咖啡

1. 這茶很好.　(Contrast: 誰要喝這杯茶?)
2. 那本字典不是漢英字典,你有漢英字典沒有?
　　我沒有,他有一本.
3. 這個人說這個好,那個人說那個好;你說哪個好?
　　這個,那個都不好.
4. 我很喜歡那兩本書,你呢?　　哪兩本書?
5. 這兩杯酒,一杯你喝,一杯我喝,好不好?
　　我不會喝,都請你喝吧.
6. 你那四位朋友都會說普通話嗎?　　兩個會,兩個不會.

(3) Indirect questions

1. 他問我誰有字典.
2. 我問他老王會說英文不會,他說不知道.
3. 他不知道哪位是王老師.

4. 我問他那是甚麼, 他說(那)是電視.
5. 你知道她為甚麼要生這麼多孩子嗎?
6. 她不說她是哪國人, 所以我們不知道她是哪國人.

(4) <u>Sentences with the pivotal construction</u>

Pattern:
Sub	Verb	Obj		
		Sub	Verb	(Obj)
誰	請	我	喝	茶 ?
我	有個朋友	姓	王	.

1. 他問我會不會說普通話.
   (Contrast: 他問我小王會不會說普通話.)
2. 我有個朋友叫老王, 他有個女兒總是喜歡說話.
3. 今天晚上他們要請我吃德國菜.
4. 有人說他有九個兒子, 八十一個孫子.　　誰?
5. 他常說沒有人不喜歡吃中國菜, 可是我就不喜歡.

家	jiā (N) home; family * a specialist in a certain field	還	hái [还] (A) still, yet; in addition
客	kè (N) guest, visitor	湯	tāng [汤] (N) soup a surname
李	lǐ * plum 李子 a common surname	瓶	píng * vase, bottle, glass jar (M) bottle of, vase of
口	kǒu (N) mouth; opening (M) for members of family; wells	錢	qián [钱] (N) money a surname
跟	gēn (C) and (CV) with; along with (V) to follow	夠	gòu [够] (SV) enough, sufficient (A) quite, pretty; enough to
的	de (K) marker of subordination	肯	kěn (MV) be willing to, agree to
買	mǎi [买] (V) to buy	行	xíng (SV) pass muster; be OK (LC) to walk; to carry out
隻	zhī [只] (M) for birds and some anim- al (among other things); one of a pair	半	bàn (半) (NU/M) half; half of 一半 (a) half 半個 half (of)...
雞	jī '鷄' [鸡] (N) chicken	准	zhǔn (V) to allow; to be allowed
條	tiáo [条] (M) for fish and various long narrow things	怎	zěn * 怎麼 how (in what manner); how come? what?
魚	yú [鱼] (N) fish	樣	yàng * [样] manner; shape (M) kind, type
青	qīng (青)* blue or green 青天 blue sky 青菜 green vegetables	抽	chōu (V) to draw out; to smoke (cigarettes,etc.)

枝	zhī (M) for pens,cigarettes, etc.	筆	bǐ　　　　　　[笔] (N) pen (M) stroke; sum of money
烟	yān '煙' (N) smoke; cigarette, 　　tobacco	用	yòng (V) to use; to employ (CV) using, by means of, 　　with
包	bāo (V) to wrap (M) a package, packet	份	fèn (M) a share; portion; copy (　　of newspaper, magazine, 　　document, etc.)
對	duì　　　　　　[对] (CV) to(wards) (SV) correct; that's right (M) pair of	報	bào　　　　　　[报] (V) to report; to requite (N) newspaper; bulletin; 　　report
起	qǐ　　　*　　[起] to rise, to raise, to begin		

32

STROKE-ORDER

家	宀 丶 丶 宀	[宀]
	豕 一 丆 丂 豕 豕 豕 豕	
客	宀	[宀]
	各 丿 夕 夂 各	
李	十 木 李	[木]
口	口	[口]
跟	𧾷 口 ⻊ ⻊ ⻊ 𧾷	[足 𧾷]
	艮 ㇆ ⺕ ⺕ 艮 艮 艮	
的	亻 白 白 白 的 的 的	[白]
買	冂 罒 罒 買 買 買 買	[貝]
(买)	乛 乛 乛 买 买 买	
隻	亻 亻 亻 隹 隻 隻 (只)	[隹]
雞	奚 丿 ⺈ ⺈ 奚 奚 奚 奚	[隹]
	隹 (鸡) ㇇ 又 又 鸡 鸡 鸡	
條	亻 亻 亻 亻 亻 攸 修 條	[木]
(条)	丿 夕 夂 条	
魚	丿 ⺈ ⺈ 角 角 角 鱼 魚 魚	[魚]
青	二 丰 丰 青 青	[青]
還	罒 罒 罒 罒 睘 睘 睘 還	[辵 辶]
(还)	一 丆 不 不 还	
湯	氵 氵 氵 氵 湯 湯 湯	[水 氵]
(汤)	氵 汤 汤 汤	
瓶	丷 丷 并 并 瓶 瓶 瓶 瓶	[瓦]
錢	金 丿 人 亼 全 全 金 金	[金 釒]
	戔 一 七 戈 戈 戋 戋 戔	
(钱)	钅 丿 𠂉 钅 钅	
	戋 一 二 戋 戋 戋	
夠	丿 ⺈ 夕 多 多 多 多 夠 夠	[夕]
(够)	丿 勹 句 够	
肯	丨 卜 止 止 肯 肯	[肉 月]
行	彳 彳 行 行	[行]
半	丶 丷 丷 兰 半	[十]
准	冫 准	[冫]
怎	丿 𠂉 乍 乍 乍 怎	[心]
樣	木 木 木 木 木 木 样 樣 樣 樣	[木]
(样)	木 木 栏 样	
抽	扌 扣 抽 抽 抽	[手 扌]
枝	木 木 朩 枝 枝	[木]
烟	丶 丷 火 火 灯 烟 烟	[火]
包	丿 勹 勺 匀 包	[勹]
對	丨 丨 业 业 业 丵 丵 丵 對 對	[寸]
(对)	㇇ 又 对 对 对	
起	十 土 丰 丰 走 走 起 起 起	[走]
筆	⺮ 𠂉 𠂉 ⺮ ⺮ ⺮	[竹 ⺮]
	聿 ㇇ ⺕ ⺕ 聿 聿 聿	
(笔)	⺮ ⺮ 笔 笔 笔	
用	丿 冂 月 用	[用]
份	亻 亻 亻 份 份	[人 亻]
報	土 去 幸 幸 報 報 報	[土]
(报)	扌 扌 护 报	

VOCABULARY

家　jiā (N) family; home

客人　kèren (N) guest

請　qǐng (V) invite

李　Lǐ (surname)

口　kǒu (M) measure for members of
family
(N) mouth

跟　gēn (C) and
(CV) along with

同學　tóngxué (N) fellow-student (can
be used as title)

的　de (K) marker of subordination

買　mǎi (V) buy

隻　zhī (M) measure for birds and
some animals (among
other things)

雞　jī (N) chicken

條　tiáo (M) measure for fish and
various long narrow
things

魚　yú (N) fish

青菜　qīngcài (N) green vegetables

還(是)　hái(shi) in addition; still,
yet

湯　tāng (N) soup

瓶　píng (M) bottle of, vase of

錢　qián (N) money

夠　gòu (SV) enough

肯　kěn (MV) be willing to, agree to

行　xíng (SV) pass muster, be OK

半　bàn (NU/M) half; half of

可以　kěyǐ (MV) be permissible;
can, may

准　zhǔn (V) allow, be allowed

怎麼樣　zěnmeyàng (IE) what's it
like? how's things? what
do you think? Well then...

貴　guì (SV) dear, expensive

那麼　nàme (IE) in that case

抽　chōu (V) draw out; smoke (
cigarettes, etc.)

烟　yān (N) smoke; cigarette, tobacco

抽烟　chōu-yān (V-O) smoke

枝　zhī (M) for pens, cigarettes, etc.

包　bāo (M) a package, packet

對不起　duìbuqǐ (IE) sorry, pardon
me, excuse me

字　zì (N) written character,
(monosyllabic) word

對　duì (SV) correct; that's right

先　xiān (A) first, in advance,
before

筆　bǐ (N) pen

用　yòng (V) use
(CV) using, by means of,
with

份　fèn (M) copy (of newspaper,
magazine, etc.)

報　bào (N) newspaper, report
(V) to report

34

老張家今天晚上有客人.他們請誰?他們請老李家.李家一共有五口兒人:老李,他愛人跟三個孩子.老張跟老李是老同學,也是很好的朋友.他們兩家的孩子也都是好朋友.老張的愛人今天想買一隻雞,一條魚跟一點兒青菜.她要做四個菜:兩個冷的,兩個熱的,還要做一個湯.老張很喜歡喝酒.他請他愛人買兩瓶.他愛人說錢不夠,不肯買.老張說請人吃飯沒酒不行,問他愛人買半條魚,買一瓶酒可不可以.他愛人說:"好吧,我買一瓶.可是晚上你不准吃魚!"

DIALOGUE

張:　怎麼樣,今天想買點兒甚麼菜?

愛:　我想買一隻雞、一條魚跟一點兒青菜;四個菜一個湯怎麼樣?

張:　好啊,幾個冷的,幾個熱的?

愛:　兩個冷的,兩個熱的.

張:　酒呢?

愛:　老李跟他愛人都不會喝酒,買酒誰喝?

張:　請人吃飯不能沒酒,買兩瓶吧!

愛:　酒那麼貴,我的錢不夠.

張:　錢不夠?! 不買魚行不行?

愛:　兩家的孩子都愛吃魚,沒魚不行!

張:　那麼,買半條魚買一瓶酒,可不可以?

愛:　好吧,我買一瓶,可是晚上你不准吃魚!

(1)

A: 怎麼樣,忙嗎? 抽枝烟吧. 我這包是法國烟.

B: 抽烟?! 對不起,請你看看那四個大字.

A: 甚麼?!"不准抽烟"!

B: 對!這個地方不准抽烟,你看看書吧.

A: 那本書是誰的? 我看看可以嗎?

B: 哪本? 是這本小書嗎?

A: 不是,是那本大的.

B: 那是老張的,你先問問他吧.

A: 這枝筆是你的吧? 我用用可以嗎?

B: 筆也是老張的.

A: 這份報也是他的嗎?

B: 報是我的,你看吧! —— 是昨天的.

(2)

A: 李先生,那位是……

B: 那位啊,他是我朋友錢漢.

A: 噢!他就是錢漢啊! 你們是老朋友吧?

B: 是啊,我們是三十年的老朋友.

A: 錢先生總是那麼忙嗎?

B: 他總是那麼忙,所以我們都叫他大忙人.

A: 有人說他不喝酒,可是你看……

B: 噢!你不知道啊?!他不喝酒是不肯喝普通的酒,今天的酒這麼好,他還肯不喝嗎?

SPEECH PATTERNS

(1) Nouns modified by other nouns

(a) more often without <u>de</u>

Pattern:　　　N　　N

我　妹妹 不喜歡做飯.

1. 他太太總是説錢不夠.

2. 老張家一共有八口兒人.

3. 他會説中國話,也能看中文報.

4. 上海人都愛吃魚嗎?

5. 他愛人不准他喝外國酒,也不准他抽外國烟.

6. 今天沒有雞湯,青菜湯行不行?　　青菜湯我不喝.

(b) usually with <u>de</u>

Pattern:　　　N　<u>de</u>　N

我妹妹的　愛人很喜歡做飯.

1. 老王的太太總是説錢不夠.

2. 我跟他是二十年的老朋友,可是不知道他是甚麼地方人.

3. 這是今天的報吧,我看看可以嗎?

4. 那不是他們家的孩子,那是他們家客人的孩子.

5a. 老張家的那兩個孩子都很好.

 b. 老張家那兩個孩子的名字都很好.

(c) where the modified noun is understood

Pattern:　這杯咖啡是誰的?

1. 哪包是你的?　　這包是我的,那包也是我的,這兩包都是我的.

2. 那兩隻雞都是他們的嗎?　　都是.

3. 這半瓶酒不是你的吧?　　不是,是我同學老王的.

4. 這份報是今天的不是?　　不是,是昨天的.

5. 對不起,這個是我的.　　你的?誰説是你的?

(2) Nouns modified by stative verbs

(a) more often without de

Pattern: SV   N

他有一個小 電視.

1. 他們冷天喝咖啡, 熱天喝茶.
2. 大魚吃小魚, 小魚吃甚麼?
3. 他沒有很多錢, 可是還要喝好酒, 抽好烟.
4. 好人很少, 好書也不多, 這話對不對?　　很對.

(b) usually with de

Pattern: SV de N

他有一個很小的電視.

1. 這是一本很普通的書, 為甚麼不准我看?
2. 為甚麼他們都想抽那麼貴的烟?
3. 我不知道他們兩個人是很好的朋友.
4. 他想買一枝不太貴的筆.

(c) where the modified noun is understood

Pattern: 大的是我的, 小的是他的.

1. 想喝甚麼? 冷的也有, 熱的也有.　　我想先喝杯茶.
2. 好的是他的, 不好的也是他的.
3. 這個是貴的, 貴的不一定好.
4. 王家的兩個女兒, 大的八歲, 小的六歲.
5. 他們家老的小的, 一共十二口兒人.

(3) Sentences with reduplicated verbs

1. 晚上想做甚麼?　　想看看電視.

2. 這是甚麼魚? 我也不知道,問問老張吧.

3. 對不起,我想問問您,這個中國話叫甚麼? 中國話叫'字典'.

4. 你會做中國菜嗎? 不會,可是很想學學.

5. 你為甚麼要請他吃飯? 他常常請我,我也應該請請他.

6. 你請我喝酒,我應該謝謝你. 不謝,不謝.

(4) Choice-type questions with two-syllable modal verbs

Patterns: a. 我可(以)不可以吃魚?
          b. 我可以吃魚不可以?

1. 你喜不喜歡喝咖啡? 很喜歡.

2. 他應不應該喝那麼多酒? 很不應該.

3. 我可不可以看看您的報? 可以,可以.

4. 我問他喜不喜歡這個地方,他不肯說.

39

明	míng * bright; clear 明天 tomorrow Míng the Ming dynasty	新	xīn (SV) new; fresh; up-to-date
日	rì * the sun; day; day of the month	聞	wén [闻] (LC) to hear (V) to smell a surname
東	dōng [东] (L) east	樂	yuè * [乐] music 音樂 a surname
西	xī (L) west 東西 thing (object, article)	現	xiàn * [现] present; current; existing; to manifest
給	gěi [给] (V) to give (CV) to; for	在	zài (V) to exist; to be in, at; to be living (CV) in; at
容	róng * to contain a surname	件	jiàn (M) piece, item
易	yì * easy; to change a surname	毛	máo (M) 1/10 of yuán 元 (N) fur; hair (of body) a surname
送	sòng (送) [送] (V) to give as a present; to deliver; to see sb. off	衣	yī * clothes

收	shōu [收]
	(V) to receive; to collect;
	     to put away
		得	děi
			(MV) have to, must; need to
			(V) to cost (money), take (
			     time)

音	yīn * sound (N) sound (in phonetics)	塊	kuài [块] (M) unit of currency; lump, piece
機	jī * [机] machine; mechanism; opportunity	便	pián * 便宜 cheap
聽	tīng [听] (V) to listen to; to hear; to obey	宜	yí * suitable; appropriate

事	shì (N) matter; job	蘋	píng * [苹] 蘋果 apple
情	qíng * feeling; affection; emotion; situation; condition	果	guǒ * fruit; result, outcome
當	dāng [当] * ought to, should (CLV) to be (in the role of), serve as	賣	mài [卖] (V) to sell

然	rán '然'
	(LC) so, thus; right, correct;
	    but, nevertheless
	當然 of course
		斤	jīn
			(M) catty (500 gr.)
			  1 斤 = 10 兩

難	nán [难] (SV) difficult	壞	huài [坏] (SV) bad; spoiled; out of order
時	shí * [时] time 小時 hour	零	líng (NU) zero, nil (AT) odd, spare
間	jiān [间] * between; among (M) for rooms 時間 time, length of time	民	mín * the people; of the people; folk; civilian

念	niàn
	(V) to read books; to read
	    aloud; to study an aca-
	    demic subject
		幣	bì '幣' * [币]
			currency
			人民幣 Renminbi (RMB)

去	qù (V) to go (to) * of last year 去年	元	yuán (M) basic unit of currency 1 元 = 10 角 = 100 分
圖	tú [图] (N) diagram; drawing; chart; map * picture	角	jiǎo [角] (M) 1/10 of yuán (written)

種	zhǒng [种]
	(M) kind, sort, type;
	    species
		分	fēn
			(M) 1/100 of yuán, cent;
			    minute (1/60 of an hour)
			(V) to divide

找	zhǎo (V) to look for; to seek; to give as change		

明	丶 刀 日 日 旫 明 明 明	[日]	當	丶 丷 丨 屵 屵 觉 觉 當	[田]
日	丨 刀 日 日	[日]	(当)	丨 丬 丬 当 当 当	
東	一 一 一 百 亘 車 東 東	[木]	然	丿 ク 夕 夕 夕 狄 狄 然	[火]
(东)	一 七 左 东 东		難	一 十 廿 廿 苫 莒 莫 難	[佳]
西	一 一 一 丙 两 西 西	[西]	(难)	刀 又 难	
給	乆 幺 幺 糸 紒 紒 給	(给)[糸]	時	日 旷 旷 旷 旿 時 時	(时) [日]
容	丶 丶 宀 宀 灾 灾 容	[宀]	間	門 間 (间)	[門]
易	日 月 易 易 易	[日]	念	人 今 念	[心]
送	丷 兰 关 关 送 (送)	[辶]	去	一 十 土 去 去	[厶]
收	丨 乚 屮 屮 屮 收 收 (收)	[攵]	圖	门 同 同 图 图 图 圖 圖	[口]
音	丶 一 一 立 音	[音]	(图)	丨 门 门 冈 冈 图 图	
機	木 朴 椣 楼 楼 機 機 (机)	[木]	種	禾 丶 一 千 禾 禾	[禾]
聽	耳 一 丁 丁 丹 耳 耳	[耳]	重	一 一 台 台 亘 重 重	
惠	十 西 悪 (听) 叿 听	(种)	禾 和 种		
新	一 立 立 辛 亲 新	[斤]	找	一 扌 扌 扌 扲 找 找	[手]
聞	門 聞 (闻) 丶 门 门 闻	[耳]	蘋	艹 苹 苹 苹 萍 莖 蘋 蘋	[艸]
樂	亻 幻 台 白 纽 幽 樂 樂	[木]	(苹)	一 十 廿 廿 芅 苹 苹	
(乐)	丿 匚 千 乐 乐		果	门 曰 日 旦 甲 早 果	[木]
現	二 千 王 玙 現 (现)	[玉]	賣	一 十 土 击 青 賣	[貝]
在	一 ナ オ 太 存 在	[土]	(卖)	一 十 土 吉 吉 卖 卖	
件	亻 亻 亻 仁 件	[人]	斤	丿 斤 斤	[斤]
毛	丿 一 二 毛	[毛]	壞	土 圹 垆 坤 壏 壞 壞 壞	[土]
衣	丶 一 ナ オ 衣 衣	[衣]	(坏)	土 圹 圷 坏 坏	
得	彳 犭 得 得 得	[彳]	零	一 一 千 雨 雨 零 零	[雨]
塊	土 圠 圴 坤 坤 塊 塊	[土]	民	丶 丆 尸 氏 民	[氏]
(块)	土 圠 圹 坎 块		幣	丬 片 片 片 散 散 幣	[巾]
便	亻 亻 𠂉 仴 便 便	[人]	(币)	丿 亻 台 币	
宜	宀 宀 宜 宜	[宀]	元	二 亍 元	[儿]
事	一 口 百 弖 写 事	[亅]	角	丿 ⺈ 门 角 角 角 (角) 角 角	[角]
情	丨 忄 忄 忄 忄 情	[心]	分	八 分 分	[刀]

42

明天　míngtiān (TW) tomorrow

生日　shēngrì (N) birthday

東西　dōngxi (N) thing (object, article)

給　gěi (V) give

容易　róngyì (SV) easy

送　sòng (V) give (as present); send, deliver; see sb. off

收音機　shōuyīnjī (N) radio receiver

聽　tīng (V) listen to

新聞　xīnwén (N) news

音樂　yīnyuè (N) music

現在　xiànzài (TW) now

件　jiàn (M) piece, item

毛衣　máoyī (N) sweater, woolly

得　děi (MV) must; need to (V) cost (money); take (time)

塊　kuài (M) unit of currency (wr. yuán 元); piece; lump

便宜　piányi (SV) cheap

事情　shìqing (N) matter; job

當然　dāngrán (MA) of course

就　jiù (A) then (introduces a con- sequence or conclusion)

難　nán (SV) difficult

有用　yǒu-yòng (SV) useful (lit: have use)

要是　yàoshi (MA) if

天天　tiāntiān (TW) day after day; everyday

時間　shíjiān (N) time

念　niàn (V) read (aloud); study an academic subject

念書　niàn-shū (V-O) study (read books)

去年　qùnián (TW) last year

地圖　dìtú (N) map, atlas

種　zhǒng (M) kind, sort, type

毛　máo (M) 1/10 of yuán 元 (wr. jiǎo 角)

找　zhǎo (V) look for; give as change

蘋果　píngguǒ (N) apple

怎麼　zěnme (QW) how? what?

賣　mài (V) sell

斤　jīn (M) catty (500 gr.)

壞　huài (SV) bad

水果　shuǐguǒ (N) fruit

兩　liǎng (M) unit of weight (=50 gr.)

零　líng (NU) zero, nil

零錢　língqián (N) change, odd coins

張　zhāng (M) sheet of

人民幣　Rénmínbì (N) 'People's Currency'

人民　rénmín (N) the people

元　yuán (M) basic unit of currency

角　jiǎo (M) 1/10 of yuán 元 (written)

分　fēn (M) 1/100 of yuán 元 , cent

PRESENTATION

　　明天是我們家老二的生日,我們想買個東西給他。老二今年十五歲,買東西給他真不容易:他喜歡的,我們不想給;我們想給的,他不一定喜歡。今年我說送他一個小收音機,可以聽聽新聞,也可以聽聽音樂。我太太說收音機太貴,現在天氣這麼冷,應該送他一件毛衣。收音機是很貴,得三十塊錢,可是毛衣也不便宜,好的也要二十多。我們家的事情,大的聽我的,小的聽我太太的;買孩子的東西當然是小事,太太說買毛衣就買毛衣吧!

DIALOGUE

A: 明天老二生日,你說買甚麼給他?

B: 買東西給他真難!

A: 是不容易!他喜歡的,我們不想給;我們想給的,他不一定喜歡。

B: 買個小收音機給他,怎麼樣?

A: 收音機太貴,我想得三十塊吧!

B: 收音機是不便宜,可是很有用:可以聽新聞,也可以聽音樂。

A: 要是他天天聽音樂,還有時間念書嗎?

B: 那麼你說買甚麼呢?

A: 買件毛衣吧。

B: 我們去年給他的不也是毛衣嗎?

A: 去年是去年,今年是今年。現在天氣這麼冷,一件毛衣夠嗎?

B: 當然不夠!好好好,你說買毛衣就買毛衣吧!

(1)　A： 您要買甚麼?

　　　B： 我這兩個孩子,老大要買一本英漢字典,老二要買一本地圖.

　　　A： 我們有兩種英漢字典:這種小的七塊半,那種大的十二塊.

　　　B： 看看可以嗎?

　　　A： 當然可以.

　　　B： 大的字多,就買大的吧.

　　　A： 好,您還要買地圖是不是?這本怎麼樣?只要六塊三毛五.

　　　B： 老二,你看看,行不行?

　　　C： 行,我們老師用的就是這種.

　　　B： 好,就買這本,一共多少錢?

　　　A： 字典十二塊,地圖六塊三毛五,一共十八塊三毛五.

　　　B： 一五、一十、十五、二十,給你二十塊.

　　　A： 謝謝,找您一塊六毛五.

(2)　A： 蘋果怎麼賣?

　　　B： 四毛五一斤,兩斤八毛,您要幾斤?

　　　A： 一斤有幾個?

　　　B： 大的一斤只有四個,小的有五個.

　　　A： 我買兩斤吧,壞的不要.

　　　B： 我們賣的水果沒有壞的,個個兒都好,兩斤二兩行不行?

　　　A： 行,多少錢?

　　　B： 八毛五.

　　　A： 我沒零錢,給你一張五塊的行嗎?

　　　B： 行,找您四塊一毛五,再見!

　　　A： 再見!

(1) Units of currency

RMB 人民幣	Spoken	Written	
Basic unit (yuán) 1/10 yuán 1/100 yuán	塊 毛 分	元 角 分	
		(a)	(b)
RMB ¥ 0.05	五分(錢)	五分	0.05
0.10	一毛(錢)	一角	0.10
0.85	八毛五(分)	八角五分	0.85
1.00	一塊(錢)	一元	1.00
1.20	一塊二(毛)/一塊兩毛	一元二角	1.20
2.50	兩塊半/兩塊五(毛)	二元五角	2.50
4.73	四塊七毛三(分)	四元七角三分	4.73
10.06	十塊零 六分	十元零 六分	10.06
10.50	十塊半/十塊五毛	十元五角	10.50
37.41	三十七塊四毛一(分)	三十七元四角一分	37.41
90.05	九十塊零 五分	九十元零 五分	90.05

Stamps:　5 分；10 分；20 分；50 分；70 分

(2) Asking prices (Amount per unit)

(a) 這本書(賣/要)多少錢?/ 幾塊錢?/ 幾毛錢?/ 幾分錢?

(b) 蘋果多少錢一斤?/ 蘋果一斤多少錢?/ 一斤蘋果多少錢?

(c) 這種烟多少錢一包?/ 這種烟一包多少錢?

(d) 蘋果怎麼賣?　1.一斤四毛五./四毛五一斤.

　　　　　　　　2.一個一毛./ 一毛一個.

酒怎麼賣?　1. 五塊半一瓶. / 一瓶五塊半.
　　　　　　2. 兩毛二一杯. / 一杯兩毛二.

魚怎麼賣?　1. 一條五毛. / 五毛一條.
　　　　　　2. 一斤八毛四. / 八毛四一斤.

(3) Goods at certain prices (noun constructions)

1a. 兩塊錢的蘋果.

b. 兩塊錢一斤的蘋果.

2a. 八塊錢的酒.

b. 八塊錢一瓶的酒.

3. 一塊錢一隻的雞.

4. 一毛錢一杯的茶.

5. 七毛五一包的烟.

(4) 'Duō' and 'bàn'

(a) duō

1. NU – M – duō

(a) 一個多 (蘋果)

(b) 兩歲多

(c) 三杯多 (酒)

(d) 四毛多 (錢)

(e) 五塊多 (錢)

(f) 五十五塊多

2. NU – duō – M

(a) 二十多位 (客人)

(b) 三十多件 (毛衣)

(c) 十多本 (地圖)

(d) 八十多枝 (筆)

(b) bàn

1. bàn – M

(a) 半瓶酒

(b) 半條魚

(c) 半斤水果

(d) 三個半條魚

2. NU – M – bàn

(a) 三隻半 (雞)

(b) 四個半

(c) 五歲半

(d) 六斤半 (蘋果)

(e) 七塊半 (錢)

(f) 九十五塊半

3. <u>yí bàn</u>

(a) 他的書,一半是英文的.

(b) 吃飯的錢,一人給一半.

(c) 他買的那五十個蘋果,一半不能吃.

(5) <u>Sentences with both direct and indirect objects</u>

Pattern:　　　S　V　indO　　dirO
　　　　　　　我 想 送　他　一點兒東西.

1. 他只肯給我兩毛錢.

2. 她沒有收音機,我們送她一個收音機怎麼樣?

3. 你想不想給他那麼多呢?　　我只想給他一半.

4. 你說送他甚麼呢?　　送他兩包烟吧.

5. 要是他不給我們東西,我們就不給他錢.

(6) <u>Modification of nouns by clauses with 'de'</u>

(a) Pattern:　　S　(MV)　V　<u>de</u>　N
　　　　　　　他　　喜歡 的 東西都很貴.

1. 你知道的(事情)真多.

2. 我看的這三本書都是老王的.

3. 我們都愛吃她做的魚.

4. 他要找的(東西)不是這個.

5. 你說的是中國話嗎?

6. 他說的那種事(情)沒人愛聽.

(b) Pattern:　　(MV)　V　O　<u>de</u>　N
　　　　　　　會 說 中國話 的 英國人多不多?

1. 愛喝酒的人一定沒錢.

2. 看報的那個人是我朋友.

3. 喜歡聽音樂的人都知道那個地方.

4. 賣書的那位老先生總是沒時間做他喜歡做的事.

5. 為甚麼買東西的人這麼多?　這個地方的東西便宜.

6. 不看報的人當然不知道這條新聞.

(c) Pattern:　　S　　　V　ind O　de　　N
　　　　　　我們去年給　他　　的　東西也是毛衣.

1. 他不太喜歡吃我們給他的那種水果.

2. 他們送我的東西沒有好的.

3. 這是他給你的錢吧?　你怎麼知道?

4. 你昨天問我的話,我現在可以問他嗎?　當然可以.

5. 老師給我們的書就是這本.

(d) Clausal expressions which have become independent nouns

1. 賣報的

2. 送報的

3. 做飯的

4. 要飯的

5. 賣魚的

6. 報新聞的

(7) Reduplication of measure words

1. 他天天晚上都要喝兩杯.

2. 我買的蘋果個個兒都是壞的.

3. 他們年年兒都要送我一瓶酒.

4. 這個地方家家都有電視.

5. 老張那五個孩子,個個兒會做飯.

6. 學中文的人天天晚上都得念書.

前	qián (L) front, front of *before; ago; former	打	dǎ (V) to hit; to fight; to play (cards and some ball games)
胖	pàng (胖) (SV) fat (of persons)	極	jí [极] *the utmost point; extreme (A) extremely, exceedingly
了	le (P) modal particle indicating change of state	拳	quán (N) fist (M) for a punch 打拳 (V-O) to box
覺	jué * [觉] to sense, to feel; to find that; to become aware	形	xíng (形) * shape, form
得	dé (V) to get; to receive (K) complement marker	完	wán (V) to finish * to be over; whole
每	měi (SP) each, every	全	quán [全] (SV) complete; whole; entire
睡	shuì (V) to sleep	瘦	shòu (SV) thin, slim; lean; tight (of clothes)
覺	jiào [觉] (N/M) a nap, a sleep 睡覺 (V-O) to sleep	精	jīng * essence; refined; skilled spirit
別	bié [别] (SP) other; different (A) = 不要 don't...(in imperative sentences)	神	shén (N) god; deity * spirit; mind
後	hòu [后] (L) back, behind, rear * after; later; afterwards	工	gōng (N) work; labour
來	lái [来] (V) to come; pro-verb standing for other verbs in context: 我不會,請你來吧!	作	zuò (V) to do; to make; to write; to compose
教	jiāo (V) to teach, to instruct 教書 (V-O) to teach	頓	dùn (頓) [顿] (M) for meals; bout of

碗	wǎn (N) bowl (M) bowl of	怕	pà (V) to fear, to dread; to be afraid that
餓	è　　　　　　[饿] (SV) hungry (V) to starve	欸	ê̄, ēi, āi (I) hey! oi!
飽	bǎo　　　　　[饱] (SV) be full, replete	認	rèn (認) * 　[认] to recognize; to acknowledge; to admit; to identify
雖	suī '雖' * 　[虽] although 雖然	識	shí　　　* 　[识] to know; to recognize; knowledge
敢	gǎn　　　　　[敢] (MV) dare to	親	qīn　　　　　[亲] * closely related; relative; intimate (V) to kiss
公	gōng　　　* public; equitable; male (of animals); metric: 公斤 kilo	身	shēn　　　* body; oneself, itself
恐	kǒng　　　* afraid; fear; terrify	體	tǐ '體' * 　[体] body; style; form; system

STROKE-ORDER

前　丷 丷 丷 肖 前 前　　　　　[刀刂]

胖　月 肝 胖 胖　　　　　　　　[肉]

了　フ 了　　　　　　　　　　　[亅]

覺　丶 丷 ⺮ 与 臼 钌 钌 钌 钌 覺 [見]

(觉)　丶 丷 ⺍ 当 覚 觉

得　彳 彴 得 得 得　　　　　　[彳]

每　一 ㇄ 与 每 每 每　　　　　[毋]

睡　目　　　　　　　　　　　　[目]

　　垂　丿 一 二 三 壬 垂 垂 垂

別　口 尸 另 別　　　　　　　　[刀刂]

(別)　口 弓 另 別

後　彳 彳 彳 移 後　　　　　　　[彳]

(后)　丶 厂 斤 后

來　一 冂 厸 杢 来 來　　　　　[人]

(来)　一 冂 三 辛 来 来

教　土 尹 考 孝　　　　　　　　[攴攵]

　　攵　丿 ㇀ 乆 攵

打　扌 打　　　　　　　　　　　[手扌]

極　木 木 栌 杨 極 極　　　　　[木]

(极)　木 朾 极 极

51

拳　ソ 兰 业 类 类 糸 拳　[手]　　雖　口 吕 咢 虽 虽 雖　[隹]
形　二 于 开 开 形 形　[彡]　　(虽)
完　宀 宁 完　[宀]　　敢　エ 于 于 퇴 耵 敢　[攵]
全　入 仝 仝 全　[入]　　(敢)　ノ エ 耳 敢
瘦　疒 ` 亠 广 疒　[疒]　　公　八 公　[八]
　　叟 ノ 亻 亻 臼 申 叟　　　恐　エ 巧 巩 巩 恐　[心]
精　ソ 业 半 半 半 精　[米]　　怕　丨 忄 忄 忄 怕 怕　[心]
神　丶 亍 礻 礻 礻 祀 神　[示]　　欽　ム 玄 乡 矢 ⺈ 欽　[欠]
工　一 丁 工　[工]　　認　言 訂 訶 認 認　[言]
作　亻 亻 仁 作 作　[人]　　(认)　讠 认
頓　丶 乚 屯 屯 屯 頓 頄 頓 [頁]　　識　言 訁 訕 語 識 識 識　[言]
(顿)　屯 屯 屯 頓 頓 頓 頓　　　(识)　讠 识
碗　石 一 厂 石　[石]　　親　亠 立 立 辛 亲 親　[見]
　　宛 宀 宀 宀 宛 宛　　　(亲)
餓　ノ 人 入 今 今 食 食 餓 [食]　　身　ノ 亻 竹 自 身 身　[身]
(饿)　ノ 勹 饣 饿　　　　體　骨 丶 冂 日 日 皿 骨　[骨]
飽　食 飣 飣 飽　[食]　　豐　冂 由 曲 典 豐 豐 豐
(饱)　饣 饱　　　　(体)　亻 体

VOCABULARY

以前　yǐqián (TW) before, previously

胖　pàng (SV) fat (of a person)

大家　dàjiā (N) everyone

胖子　pàngzi (N) fat person

了　le (P) modal particle indicating change of state

覺得　juéde (V) to feel, sense

每　měi (SP) each, every

睡覺　shuì-jiào (V-O) sleep

別(的)　bié(de) (SP) other, alternative

後來　hòulái (MA) afterwards, later on (refers to past events)

教　jiāo (V) teach

教書　jiāo-shū (V-O) teach

52

打　dǎ (V) hit; fight; play (cards and some ball games)

太極拳　tàijíquán (N) a form of exercise remotely resembling shadow-boxing

情形　qíngxing (N) situation, state of affairs

完全　wánquán (SV/A) complete; completely

一樣　yíyàng (SV/A) the same; equally

瘦　shòu (SV) thin, slim

精神　jīngshen (N) spirit, vitality (SV) spruce, smart, lively

工作　gōngzuò (N) work (V) to work

頓　dùn (M) meal; bout; spell

碗　wǎn (N/M) bowl; bowl of

餓　è (SV) be hungry

飽　bǎo (SV) be full, replete

雖然　suīrán (MA) although

本來　běnlái (MA) originally, in the first place

敢　gǎn (MV) dare to

公斤　gōngjīn (M) kilo (gōng, prefix for metric units)

再　zài (A) again; further, progressively

恐怕　kǒngpà (MA) I'm afraid; perhaps

欸　ē̌, ēi, āi (I) hey! oi!

認識　rènshi (V) recognize; know

那　nà (MA) then, in that case (= 那麼)

父親　fùqin (N) father

做事　zuò-shì (V-O) work (not limited to occupation)

母親　mǔqin (N) mother

身體　shēntǐ (N) body; health

怕　pà (V) fear, dread; be afraid of

老孫的朋友小王以前很胖,大家都叫他胖子.很多人只知道他叫胖子,不知道他姓甚麼、叫甚麼.小王因為太胖了,總是覺得累.每天只想吃飯睡覺,不想做別的事.後來有位朋友教他打太極拳,情形就完全不一樣了:人也瘦了,精神也好了.以前不喜歡工作,現在他一個人做兩個人的事;以前每頓吃五碗飯還覺得餓,現在兩碗就飽了.老孫雖然人不胖,也常常覺得精神不好,他本來很想學學太極拳,可是現在不敢了.小王問他為甚麼,他說:"你本來很胖,打打太極拳就瘦了,當然很好,我現在只有四十多公斤,要是再瘦恐怕我這個人就沒有了!"

DIALOGUE

王： 欸,老孫,你不認識我了?我是小王啊!

孫： 甚麼?! 胖子小王?你怎麼....

王： 瘦了,是不是?

孫： 是啊,你以前不是很胖嗎?

王： 以前是很胖,有八十五公斤,現在天天打太極拳,只有六十公斤了.人瘦了,精神也好了.

孫： 我人雖然很瘦,可是常常覺得累,沒精神.

王： 你也可以打打太極拳啊!

孫： 我本來很想學學,可是現在不敢了.

王： 為甚麼?

孫： 你本來很胖,打打太極拳就瘦了,當然很好.我現在只有四十多公斤,要是再瘦,恐怕我這個人就沒有了!

SKETCHES

(1)

A: 早啊!

B: 早!天氣冷了.

A: 是啊,買東西的人也少了.

B: 買東西的人少了,不是因為天氣冷吧?

A: 那是因為甚麼?

B: 恐怕是因為東西貴了.

A: 東西是貴了.去年蘋果三毛二一斤,現在五毛四了.

B: 昨天魚賣八毛五一斤,今天賣一塊了.

A: 東西貴了,可是我們的錢還是一樣.

B: 所以現在每頓我只能吃一碗飯了!

(2)

A: 怎麼樣,你們都好嗎?

B: 都好,你們呢?

A: 我們也都好,你父親還做事嗎?

B: 他現在太老了,不能工作了.

A: 是不是還愛喝兩杯?

B: 酒這麼貴,他也不常喝了.

A: 烟還抽嗎?

B: 我媽不准他抽,他也不敢抽了.

A: 你母親身體還那麼好吧?

B: 她現在怕胖,不敢吃東西,所以身體不那麼好了.

A: 你妹妹還教書嗎?

B: 她不教了.她說教書這種工作太累了.

SPEECH PATTERNS

(1) Sentences with modal particle 'le' indicating change of state

(a) Pattern: SV le
他以前很瘦,現在怎麼這麼胖了?

1. 中文很難嗎?   我現在覺得不太難了.
2. 王家有幾個孩子?   兩個,都大了.
3. 蘋果壞了嗎?   他買的十公斤蘋果都壞了!
4. 會說普通話的人多不多?   以前很少,現在多了.
5. 買個小收音機得多少錢?   現在便宜了,二十五塊就夠了.
6. 現在你還餓嗎?   不餓了.

(b) Pattern: (neg) V (O) le
他怎麼不學中文了?

1. 再吃一塊魚吧!   不了,謝謝您,我不吃了.
2. 他不怕他父親嗎?   以前很怕,現在不太怕了.
3. 您還有別的事嗎?   沒有了.
4. 你的好朋友老張怎麼樣?   老張?! 他不是我的朋友了.
5. 他們有八個孩子,還要生嗎?   他們說不生了,誰知道!
6. 你們吃飯吧,不要說話了!   好,不說了.

(c) Pattern: MV V   (O) le
他不敢學太極拳了.

1. 你會打太極拳嗎?   以前會,現在不會了.
2. 他喜歡聽音樂嗎?   以前不太喜歡,現在很喜歡了.
3. 他們家的孩子都愛看電視嗎?   現在大了,不那麼愛看了.
4. 電視這麼貴,你不想買了吧?   不想買了,有個收音機就行了.
5. 你們都會說中國話了吧?
都會說一點兒了,可是還不認識中國字.
6. 你怎麼不喝了?   晚上得教書,不能再喝了.

56

(d) The three above patterns illustrated by means of contrast

1a. 青菜便宜,雞跟魚都很貴.
 b. 天氣熱了,青菜便宜了.

2a. 他們只賣書,不賣地圖.
 b. 買地圖的人少了,他們不賣地圖了.

3a. 他是老李的朋友,我不認識他.
 b. 小王現在這麼胖,我完全不認識他了.

4a. 她想學新聞,不想學音樂.
 b. { 她本來想學音樂,現在不想學了.
     她本來學音樂,現在不想學了.

5a. 她愛人沒有工作,他們沒有錢.
 b. 他們以前很有錢,可是天天吃好的,喝好的,後來就沒有錢了.

6a. 他父親是胖子,他不是胖子.
 b. 他現在只有四十公斤了,不是胖子了.

(2) Modal particle 'le' used to show 'excessiveness'

1. 小張(有)八十五公斤,太胖了.
2. 這種收音機太普通了,家家都有.
3. 他做的那種工作太容易了,我也會做.
4. 對不起,我太累了,我想睡覺了.
5. 他太愛看電視了,沒有一天晚上不看.
6. 我太想吃魚了,今天能不能買一條?
7. 他一個人做十個人的事,精神太好了.
8. 謝謝您,我太飽了,不能再吃了!

(3) Sentences with adverbs used as correlative conjunctions

(a)　只 ….. 不/沒 …..

　　1. 他只會說,不會做.
　　2. 這個地方只有咖啡,沒有茶.
　　3. 他們只賣魚,不賣別的.
　　4. 只准他打人,不准人打他.

(b)　也 ….. 也 …..

　　1. 大家都想學英文,我們也想學,他們也想學.
　　2. 他喜歡吃外國菜;法國菜也吃,德國菜也吃.
　　3. 天氣好,我們也工作;天氣不好,我們也工作.
　　4. 這個地方只有這種水果;你吃也可以,不吃也可以.

(c)　雖然 ….. 可是…..

　　1. 雖然他父母親都是中國人,可是他不會說中國話.
　　2. 東西雖然很貴,可是還有很多人買.
　　3. 工作雖然很忙,可是大家的精神都很好.
　　4. 我雖然每天看報,可是不看這種新聞.

(d)　要是 ….. 就…..

　　1. 要是他肯說說那天的情形,那就太好了.
　　2. 要是你不准我看電視,我就不准你聽收音機.
　　3. 這麼做恐怕不行吧?　要是他說行就行.
　　4. 要是你沒零錢,就給我一張十塊的吧.

(e)　因為….. 所以…..

　　1. 因為他有很多中國朋友,所以想學點兒中文.
　　2. 因為她太愛聽音樂了,所以沒時間念書.
　　3. 他因為身體不好,所以很怕晚上工作.
　　4. 他賣的水果都是壞的,所以沒人買.

58

南	nán (L) south	左	zuǒ (L) left, to/on the left a surname
山	shān (N) mountain, hill	右	yòu (L) right, to/on the right
社	shè (N) organized body, society; agency 公社 commune	邊	biān [边] (N) side; border; edge (L-suffix) side
象	xiàng (象) * appearance; image; phenom- enon (N) elephant	竹	zhú * bamboo 竹子
站	zhàn (V) to stand (N) station; (bus) stop	風	fēng [风] (N) wind
最	zuì (A) most, exceedingly (used to form superlative)	景	jǐng * scene, scenery, view
裏	lǐ '裡' [里] (L) in, inside	近	jìn [近] (SV) near, close; intimate
員	yuán [员] (N/M) member of group, trade, profession 社員 commune member	寫	xiě [写] (V) to write; to compose
房	fáng * house 房子 ; room (as in 客房 guest room, 書房 study)	信	xìn (V) to believe; to believe in (N) letter; message
頭	tóu [头] (N) head (L-suffix) top; end (SP) first	城	chéng (N) city wall; city
湖	hú (N) lake	玩	wán (V) to play; to have fun, to amuse oneself
樹	shù [树] (N) tree (M:棵 kē) * to set up	決	jué [决] * to decide, to determine (A) definitely (not)

第	dì '第' (prefix) ordinal prefix 第一 first; 第二 second	下	xià (L) below; down; under; underneath (SP) next (V) to descend; to alight
次	cì (M) time; occasion * inferior, second-rate	廣	guǎng '廣' [广] (SV) broad; wide; vast 廣東 Guangdong (Kwangtung)
路	lù (N) road, path; way, route	部	bù (N) part, section; govt.dept. (L-suffix) part, section (M) for films, machines, etc.
走	zǒu (V) to go; to leave; to walk	桌	zhuō '棹' * table 桌子 (M:張)
理	lǐ (N) reason; principle; logic (V) to put in order	椅	yǐ * chair 椅子 (M:把 bǎ/張)
快	kuài (SV) quick, fast; sharp (of knives) (A) quickly, very soon	底	dǐ (N) bottom
到	dào (V) to arrive; to reach (CV) to; up until	旁	páng * side; other; lateral radical of a Chinese character
向	xiàng * towards; to be partial to; direction		

STROKE-ORDER

南	一 十 十 冇 南 南 南	[十]	(里)	口 曰 旦 甲 里	
山	丨 山 山	[山]	員	口 肙 冒 員	[口]
社	丶 亍 亍 オ 礻 礻 社	[示]	(员)	口 员	
象	ク 宀 缶 缶 多 多 多 象 象	[豸]	房	丶 宀 亡 户 户 房 房	[户]
站	丶 亠 立 剆 圠 站	[立]	頭	口 豆 豇 頭	[頁]
最	日 旦 晜 晜 昮 最	[日]	(头)	二 头 头	
裏	亠 亠 亩 亩 重 享 喪 裏 裏	[衣]	湖	氵 沽 湖	[水]

60

<u>VOCABULARY</u>

南 nán (L) south

山 shān (N) mountain, hill

公社 gōngshè (N) commune

氣象 qìxiàng (N) meteorology, weather

站 zhàn (N) station; (bus) stop
(V) to stand

最 zuì (A) most; exceedingly (used to form superlative)

在 zài (V/CV) to be located in/at

裏 lǐ (L) in

員 yuán (N) member of group, trade, profession

氣象員 qìxiàngyuán (N) weatherman

所(兒) suǒ(r) (M) classifier for houses and some buildings

房子 fángzi (N) house

頭 tóu (N/L-suffix) head; top

前頭 qiántou (L/PW) in front

湖 hú (N) lake

後頭 hòutou (L/PW) behind

樹 shù (N) tree

左　zuǒ (L) left, to/on the left

右　yòu (L) right, to/on the right

邊(兒)　biān(r) (N/L-suffix) side

竹子　zhúzi (N) bamboo

風景　fēngjǐng (N) scenery

美　měi (SV) beautiful

近　jìn (SV) near, close

　　最近　zuìjìn (TW) (just) recently

寫　xiě (V) write

信　xìn (N) letter

城　chéng (N) city wall; city

　　城裏　chéng-li (PW) in town; urban

去　qù (V) to go, go to

玩(兒)　wán(r) (V) to play; to amuse oneself

決定　juédìng (V) decide
　　　　　　(N) decision

第　dì-(prefix) ordinal prefix

　　第一　dìyī (prefix + NU) first

次　cì (M) time; occasion

路　lù (N) road, path; way, route

走　zǒu (V) to go, to leave; to walk

　　走路　zǒu-lù (V-O) to walk

地理　dìlǐ (N) geography

快　kuài (SV) quick, fast
　　　　(A) quickly; very soon

到　dào (V) to arrive, reach
　　　　(CV) to

上　shàng (L) top; on top of; above

北　běi (L) north

　　北邊(兒)　běibian(r) (L/PW) north

哪邊(兒)　něibian(r) (QW) where? (which side?)

方向　fāngxiàng (N) direction

那邊(兒)　nèibian(r) (L/PW) there (that side)

小孩(兒)　xiǎohái(r) (N) child

哪兒　nǎr (PW) where? (= nǎlǐ?)

下　xià (L) below; down; under; underneath

西　xī (L) west

東　dōng (L) east

地名　dìmíng (N) place name

部　bù (N/L-suffix) part, section

　　南部　nánbù (PW) southern part, the south

那兒　nàr, nèr (L/PW) there (= nàlǐ)

這兒　zhèr (L/PW) here (= zhèlǐ)

桌子　zhuōzi (N) table

椅子　yǐzi (N) chair

底下　dǐxia (L/PW) under; below; beneath

中間　zhōngjiān
中間兒　zhōngjiànr } (L/PW) between; among; in the middle

旁邊(兒)　pángbiān(r) (L/PW) (by) the side of

女的　nǚ-de (N) female

外　wài (L) outside

南山人民公社一共有五個氣象站.最小的那個在大山裏,只有一個氣象員叫小張是我的老同學.這個氣象站雖然只是一所兒普通的房子,可是前頭有湖,後頭有樹,左右兩邊兒都是竹子,風景很美.小張很喜歡這個地方.可是他一個人在山裏,沒有朋友.最近寫信給我跟小王,請我們這兩個城裏人去玩兒.昨天天氣很好,我跟小王決定去看看他.我們兩個人都是第一次去.大家都說山裏的路不好找,本來應該先問問別人怎麼走,小王說他有地圖,看地圖就行了.他是學地理的,我當然得聽他的,可是.....

DIALOGUE

A: 小王,我太餓了.不能再走了!

B: 快到了,快到了.欸!地圖上怎麼沒有這所兒房子啊?

A: 氣象站應該在北邊兒,可是哪邊兒是北啊?

B: 我現在也不知道方向了.欸!你看,那邊兒有個小孩兒,我們去問問他.

A: 小朋友,這是甚麼地方?

C: 這是我家.

B: 這山裏是不是有個氣象站?

C: 我們老師說有.

A: 你知道在哪兒嗎?

C: 我們老師說就在湖邊兒.

B: 哪個湖邊兒?那個湖在甚麼地方呢?

C: 我們老師說那個湖叫小明湖,在北邊兒.

A: 那麼,你知道哪邊兒是北嗎?

C: 你看你的地圖吧,我們老師說,上北下南,左西右東,地圖的上邊兒就是北!

SKETCHES

(1)

A: 我想問你兩個中國地名好不好？

B: 我知道一點兒中國地理,你問吧！

A: 山東在哪兒?

B: 山東在山西的東邊兒.

A: 湖南呢?

B: 湖南在湖北的南邊兒.

A: 廣西呢?

B: 廣西在廣東的西邊兒.

A: 可是廣東在哪兒呢?

B: 廣東當然在廣西的東邊兒.

A: 這我也知道,我要問的是廣東在中國甚麼地方?

B: 不是在中國的南部嗎?

(2)

A: 今天的報在你那兒嗎?

B: 不在我這兒,是不是在你後頭的桌子上?

A: 沒有啊！噢!在這兒,在椅子底下.

B: 我今天還沒時間看報,有甚麼新聞?

A: 報上說東西都貴了.

B: 那不是新聞!

A: 最近找工作很難了.

B: 那也不是新聞! 欸!快,快,你看!電視上這三個人,中間那個是不是小李?

A: 是小李,他旁邊兒那個女的是誰?

B: 不認識,我不知道他有一位這麼好看的女朋友.

SPEECH PATTERNS

(1) Directions and place words

(a) Compass directions

東	E	東 南	SE
南	S	東 北	NE
西	W	西 南	SW
北	N	西 北	NW

(b) Relative place words

上頭 / 上邊	東邊兒
下頭 / 下邊	南邊兒
裏頭 / 裏邊	西邊兒
外頭 / 外邊	北邊兒
前頭 / 前邊	東南邊兒
後頭 / 後邊	西北邊兒
左邊	北部
右邊	東南部
中間 / 中間兒	這邊～這裏 = 這兒
底下	那邊～那裏 = 那兒
	哪邊?～哪裏? = 哪兒?

(c) Place-word phrases

房子(的)前頭/邊	氣象站(的)北邊
大山(的)後頭/邊	英國(的)南邊
城外頭/邊; 城外	中國(的)西北部
湖裏頭/邊; 湖裏	我這兒
樹(的)上頭/邊; 樹上	你那兒
山(的)下頭/邊; 山下	老王那兒
你(的)左邊	書上
地圖(的)右邊	信上
樹(的)底下	報上
路(的)中間/中間兒	字典裏

(2) 'Zài' as main verb with complement

Pattern:　　N　　_zài_　　PW

報　在　哪兒？　在桌子上。

1. 你家在哪兒？　　我家在城外頭。
2. 有人在家嗎？　　哪位？
3. 你說的那所兒房子在哪兒？　　就在東湖南邊兒。
4. 他工作的地方在城裏頭嗎？　　不在城裏頭，在山上。
5. 她給我的信在哪兒？　　就在桌子上，字典旁邊兒。
6. 你的錢呢？　　都在我愛人那兒！
7. 方向對嗎？　　對，你看西湖不是在我們左邊兒嗎？

(3) Existence in a place

Pattern:　　PW　　_yǒu_　　N

中國　有　很多大山。

1. 英國北部有沒有大湖？　　有，有不少風景很美的大湖。
2. 山上有很多房子，每所兒房子前頭都有蘋果樹。
3. 桌子上有杯茶，不知道是誰的。
4. 東湖西邊兒有一條大路，路的兩邊兒都是竹子。
5. 城裏有個賣魚的地方，那兒的魚很便宜。
6. 我這兒沒有他要的那個東西。
　　Contrast: 我沒有他要的那個東西。

(4) Collocations including PW suffixes

1. 報上沒有這個新聞。
2. 書上說這種竹子只有中國有。
3. 字典裏沒有這個字嗎？　　沒有。
4. 他信上說最近工作很忙，可是身體很好。
5. 我這張地圖上有兩個西山。
6. 收音機上說最近買房子的人少了。

(5) Modification by place expressions

1. 房子後頭的樹都是蘋果樹嗎?
2. 老張旁邊兒的那個女的是誰?　　那是他妹妹.
3. 我很喜歡湖中間兒的那所兒小房子.
4. 椅子上的那本地理書是誰的?
5. 他最想吃的就是西湖裏的魚.
6. 你每天晚上都看電視上的新聞嗎?

(6) The particle 'le' indicating imminent action

1. 北京快到了嗎?　　快了! 快了!
2. 我要睡覺了, 不能再吃了.
3. 他幾歲?　　快八歲了.
4. 難不難?　　不太難, 我快會了.
5. 他的生日就要到了, 你決定送他甚麼?
6. 新聞時間快到了, 我們聽聽新聞吧!
7. 天氣快要冷了, 我得去買毛衣了.

(7) Stative verbs as adverbs

1. 他家在城裏頭, 很容易找.
2. 中文很難學嗎?　　不難學!
3. 中國菜好吃, 可是不好做. (= 難做)
4. 這件事很難決定嗎?　　很難決定, 我們問問別的人吧.
5. 湖邊兒的風景真好看.
6. 這個音樂很好聽.
7. 他送我的那瓶酒不好喝.
8. 老王請客, 人多菜少, 不夠吃.
9. 我想寫信問問他北京有甚麼好玩兒的地方.

67

傅	fù * tutor, teacher 師傅 master worker, skilled craftsman	店	diàn (N) shop, store; inn
鐵	tiě [铁] (N) iron	售	shòu * (LC) to sell, to retail
廠	chǎng '厰' [厂] (N) factory, mill, plant	弟	dì * younger brother 弟弟
男	nán * man, male (of persons)	農	nóng * [农] agriculture, farming 農民 peasant
已	yǐ (A) already (LC) to cease	搞	gǎo (V) to do; to make; to go in for; to set up; to get hold of
經	jīng * [经] to pass through; to undergo; a sacred book, classic	利	lì (N) advantage; profit, interest * favourable; to benefit
解	jiě [解] (V) to undo; to liberate * to explain; to solve	幹	gàn [干] (V) to do, to work * trunk; main part 幹部 cadre
放	fàng (V) to let go; to let out/off; to place	錯	cuò [错] (SV) wrong, mistaken (N) fault, error 不錯 that's right; not bad
軍	jūn [军] army, armed forces; military 軍人 serviceman	化	huà (V) to change, transform; to melt * -ize, -ify
百	bǎi (NU) hundred	平	píng (SV) flat, level, even, smooth
貨	huò [货] (N) goods, commodity	高	gāo '髙' (SV) high; tall a surname
商	shāng * trade, commerce, business; to discuss, to consult the Shang dynasty	哥	gē * elder brother 哥哥

着	zháo [着] (V) to touch * to catch; to suffer; to be troubled with	單	dān * [单] single; odd; singly; only; alone; list (as in 名單 name list, 菜單 menu)
急	jí (急) (SV) hurried; worried; impatient; irritated; urgent	像	xiàng (象) [象] (V) to resemble (SV) similar, alike (N) portrait; statue
語	yǔ * [语] speech; language; dialect 漢語 the Chinese language	產	chǎn '產' * [产] to produce, to yield; product; property; real estate
替	tì (V) to substitute for; to take the place of (CV) for; on behalf of	隊	duì (隊) [队] (N) team; group (M) for groups of men, warships, aeroplanes, etc.
星	xīng (N) star	介	jiè * be situated between
期	qī * a period of time; scheduled time 星期 week (M) an issue	紹	shào * [绍] to continue; to connect
辦	bàn [办] (V) to do, handle, manage; to see to; to punish (by law)	安	ān * peaceful; quiet; safe (V) to install; to fix on
久	jiǔ (SV) long protracted (time)	局	jú * bureau, office; situation (M) for games, sets, innings (of chess, tennis, etc.)

STROKE-ORDER

傅   亻 佇 佑 俌 傅 傳 傅   [人]   (经)   纟 纟 纩 纩 经

鐵   金 亼 仐 仐 金 金   [金]   解   角 角 角 卻 卻 解 解(解)   [角]

   釯 鈷 鐘 鐵 鐵 鐵   放   亠 宀 方 放   [攴]

(铁)   丿 ヒ 牟 钅 钅 铣 铁   軍   冖 冖 冒 宣 軍   [車]

廠   一 广 庐 庐 庿 廠 (厂)   [广]   (军)   冖 冖 冇 军 军

男   冂 冂 田 田 甼 男   [田]   百   一 丆 丆 万 百 百   [白]

己   フ コ 己   [己]   貨   亻 仁 化 貨 (货)   [貝]

經   糸 紅 紅 經 經 經   [糸]   商   亠 亠 产 商 商   [口]

店 `丶 亠 广 庐 庐 店` [广]	語 `言 訁 訂 訊 評 語` (语) [言]
售 `亻 仁 仹 隹 售` [口]	替 `二 夫 扶 扶 替` [曰]
弟 `丷 丬 当 肖 弟 弟` [弓]	星 `日 旦 旦 星 星` [日]
農 `曲 曲 曲 曲 農 農 農 農` [辰]	期 `一 艹 甘 其 期` [月]
(农) `一 少 𠂤 农 农`	辦 `丷 立 立 辛 辦 辦 辦 辦 辦 辦` [辛]
搞 `扌 扩 护 搞 搞` [手]	(办) `フ カ 办 办`
利 `二 千 禾 禾 利 利` [刀]	久 `丿 夂 久` [丿]
幹 `十 古 卓 乾 乾 幹` (干) [干]	單 `丷 吅 吅 單 單` (单) [口]
錯 `金 釒 釒 鉔 錯` (错) [金]	像 `亻 伫 伫 侉 傳 傳 像` (象) [人]
化 `亻 仁 化` [匕]	產 `亠 亠 产 产 產 產` (产) [生]
平 `一 丂 平` [干]	隊 `阝 阼 阼 阵 隊 隊` (队) [阜]
高 `亠 古 高 高` [高]	介 `人 介 介` [人]
哥 `一 丂 可 可 哥 哥` [口]	紹 `纟 纩 紗 紹` (绍) [糸]
着 `丷 半 半 羊 羊 着` (著) [目]	安 `宀 宀 安 安` [宀]
急 `丿 勹 刍 刍 刍 急` [心]	局 `フ コ コ 尸 尸 局` [尸]

VOCABULARY

師傅 shīfu (N) master craftsman; old hand

鐵 tiě (N) iron

(工)廠 (gōng)chǎng (N) factory, works, mill

工人 gōngrén (N) worker, workman

小學 xiǎoxué (N) junior school

男 nán (AT) male

已經 yǐjing (A) already

解放軍 jiěfàngjūn (N) Liberation Army; member of same

解放 jiěfàng (V) liberate (N) liberation

百貨商店 bǎihuò shāngdiàn (N) 'hundred goods shop', i.e. (department) store

(商)店 (shāng)diàn (N) shop, store

當 dāng (CLV) be (in position of), serve as

售貨員 shòuhuòyuán (N) 'sell goods person'— shop assistant

姐妹 jiěmèi (N) sisters (older and younger)

弟弟 dìdi (N) younger brother

大學 dàxué (N) university

農 nóng (N) agriculture

搞 gǎo (V) do, go in for, make, get up to

70

水利 shuǐlì (N) water conservancy

幹部 gànbù (N) cadre

錯 cuò (N) mistake
      (SV) wrong, in error

   不錯 bú-cuò (IE) that's right;
          not bad, pretty good

文化 wénhuà (N) culture; (standard
              of) education

水平 shuǐpíng (N) level, standard

高 gāo (SV) high; tall

對象 duìxiàng (N) object (of affec-
              tion); girlfriend or
              boyfriend

做 zuò (CLV) be, act as, serve as

哥哥 gēge (N) elder brother

為 wèi (CV) because of, for the sake
           of

著急 zháojí (V) worry about
          (SV) anxious, worried

外語 wàiyǔ (N) foreign language

替 tì (CV) on behalf of, for
        (V) to stand in for

星期日/天 xīngqī-rì/tiān (TW)
              Sunday

   星期 xīngqī (N) week

給 gěi (CV) for; in the interests of

辦 bàn (V) do, manage, see to

   辦事 bàn shì (VO) see to matters,
                   business

好久不見 hǎo jiǔ bú jiàn (IE)
              long time no see

單位 dānwèi (N) unit; place of work

好像 hǎoxiàng (MA) seemingly, as if

生產隊 shēngchǎnduì (N) production
                      team

   生產 shēngchǎn (V) produce
                  (N) production

大隊 dàduì (N) 'big team'— brigade

機會 jīhuì (N) opportunity

介紹 jièshao (V) introduce
            (N) introduction

   給人介紹 gěi rén jièshao (PH)
              effect an introduction
              for somebody

晚 wǎn (SV) late

(是)真的 (shì) zhēn de (SV) be true

書店 shūdiàn (N) bookshop

人民日報 Rénmín Rìbào (PR) People's
                      Daily

公安局 gōng'ānjú (N) public security
                    bureau

別 bié (= 不要) don't (negative
                imperative)

叫 jiào (V) tell; order

中學 zhōngxué (N) middle school

問 X 好 wèn X hǎo (IE) ask after, give
                regards to X

　　李師傅是我們城裏一個鐵工廠的老工人,他愛人在第八小學教書,他們有兩個孩子,一男一女,都已經二十多了.男孩子是解放軍,不常在家,女孩子在百貨商店當售貨員.老李沒有姐妹,只有一個弟弟叫李明道,以前在大學學農,現在在青山人民公社搞水利,是個幹部,人很不錯,文化水平也高,可是今年已經三十五了,還沒有對象,因為父母親都不在了,這個做哥哥的常常為這件事着急.最近弟弟想學外語,寫信請哥哥替他在城裏買兩本書.今天星期日,老李就去給弟弟辦這件事,在路上……

DIALOGUE

王: 欸!李師傅,好久不見,還認識我嗎?

李: 小王!當然認識,好久不見!現在在哪個單位工作啊?

王: 三〇六廠,還是當工人.

李: 那好啊,有幾個孩子了?

王: 兩個,一男一女,不能再生了.

李: 欸,小王,你好像有個妹妹,是不是?

王: 是啊,現在在青山公社.

李: 青山公社?!我弟弟也在青山啊,你妹妹在哪個生產隊?

王: 好像是東湖大隊.

李: 太好了!我弟弟也在東湖,有機會能不能給他們介紹介紹,我弟弟還沒….

王: 太晚了!我妹妹已經有對象了.

李: 噢?!真的?!

王: 當然是真的,她對象也姓李,就在他們社裏搞水利,好像叫李明道.

李: 甚麼?!李明道!那不就是我弟弟嗎!

(1)

A: 好久不見,家裏人都好吧?

B: 都好,最近還是那麼忙嗎?

A: 一樣,欸,你哥哥現在在哪個單位工作啊?

B: 在二中教書.

A: 你姐姐呢?

B: 在新華書店當售貨員.

A: 你弟弟還在二〇四廠嗎?

B: 不,他不在工廠了,現在是我們社裏的氣象員,在山上工作.

A: 你妹妹不在人民日報了吧?

B: 還在,她就喜歡搞新聞工作.

A: 你知道我現在在哪個單位嗎?

B: 不知道.噢!我知道了,是不是在公安局?

(2)

A: 不早了,我得走了!

B: 別走了,就在我們這兒吃飯吧!

A: 不了,謝謝,我還得去給我妹妹買東西.

B: 他們還在山上嗎?

A: 是啊,她說山上已經冷了,叫我替她買件毛衣.

B: 他們有幾個孩子了?

A: 三個了,都還小,天天為這三個孩子忙.

B: 她愛人呢?

A: 她愛人最近替朋友在城裏的中學教書,很少在家.

B: 現在大家好像都很忙,你要是寫信,請你替我問他們好!

(1) Verbal expressions in series

(a) First verb as functive verb
(the verbs in series are marked by dots)

1. 明天是我們家老二的生日,我們想買個東西給他.

2. (他)寫信給我跟小王,請我們這兩個城裏人去玩兒.

3. 晚上有客人我得去買菜.

4. 他想做頓法國菜吃.

5. 你為甚麼不買瓶好酒喝?

6. 山裏沒人,他很想找個朋友說話.

7. 他父母要送他去學農,可是他想學音樂.

8. 他那兒沒有書店,他寫信請他哥哥替他買書.

9. 第五中學要找人教外語,你可以介紹我去嗎?

10. 你們有飯吃,有書念,還要甚麼?

(b) First verb as coverb
(the coverbs are marked by dots)

1. 對不起,這兒不准說上海話,請你用普通話說.

2. 星期三我不能去,請你替我跟老師說一說.

3. 他給的錢太少了,沒人肯給他做事.

4. 誰給這三個孩子做飯?

5. 你想跟誰學中文?

6. 我不愛跟那種人說話.

7. 你怎麼能用你父母給你買書的錢買酒喝呢?　我知道我錯了.

8. 請你替我用中國話跟他們說一說,好不好?

9. 你三十五了,還沒對象,我真為你着急!

10. 別着急了,給我介紹一位女朋友就行了.

11. 不准給他寫信:　　a. 不准寫信給他.
　　　　　　　　　　b. 不准替他寫信.

74

(2) 'Zài' as coverb giving setting for main action

Pattern:　　S　zài　PW　V　(O)
他　在　小學　教書.

1. 今天晚上沒事,我想在家看看書、寫寫信.

2. 張家的老二、老三都在二中念書嗎?　　不錯,都在二中.

3. 你喜歡在外國工作嗎?　　這很難說.

4. 天氣太熱了,很多人在房子外頭睡覺.

5. 他想在城外搞個小工廠.

6. 孩子們好像都愛在海邊玩兒.

7. 她不在那個商店買東西,她說那兒的東西貴.

8. 在城裏找工作很不容易,機會太少了.

9. 他說那個地方就在上海的西南邊兒,請你在地圖上找找.

10a. 他不在家喝酒. (他在哪兒喝酒? 在家喝嗎?)

　b. 他在家不喝酒. (他在家喝不喝酒?)

(3) Modification of nouns by clauses containing place expressions

Pattern:　　zài　PW　V　O　de　N
在　商店　買東西　的　人

1. 那天在你家吃飯的那位先生是不是學農的?

2. 在這個大學教書的老師都是英國人嗎?

3. 沒有人認識那位在那兒喝酒的老太太.

4. 在樹上吃蘋果的那兩個孩子是誰家的?

5. 在東湖前邊賣報的那個人以前是學新聞的.

6. 我很想知道那位天天在大學前邊打太極拳的老先生多少歲了.

7. 那位就是在我們公社搞水利的李師傅.以前是解放軍.

8. 我那位在公安局工作的朋友外語水平很高,也很會辦事.

75

(4) <u>Classifactory verbs relating to job, status, function, etc.</u>

1. 他兩個弟弟都在第一鐵工廠當工人.
2. 很多人都想當百貨商店的售貨員.
3. 在這兒當老師的都喜歡喝酒嗎?
4. 小王想當解放軍,可是不夠高.
5. 做父母的誰不愛兒女?
6. 老王說話很不好聽,沒人喜歡跟他做朋友.
7. 做客人的當然不能說菜不好吃.

(5) <u>Subject-predicate predicates</u>

1. 他哥哥人好像不錯.
2. 他弟弟身體不錯,人也精神.
3. 我妹妹念書好,辦事不行.
4. 老張人高,文化也高.
5. 中國地大人多.
6. 這地方前頭有湖,後頭有山,風景真不錯.
7. 他愛人做的菜,雞好吃,魚不好吃.
8. 今天星期天,每個商店人都很多.
9. 山上樹多,房子少.
10a. 他妹妹工作好.
  b. 他妹妹的工作好.

倫	lún　　　*　　[伦] human relationships	談	tán　　　　　[谈] (V) to talk, chat, discuss, 　　negotiate 談天兒 to chat
敦	dūn　　　* honest, sincere 倫敦 London	題	tí　　　　　[题] * topic, subject, title (V) to inscribe
館	guǎn 馆ɪ　　[馆] (N) house; establishment; hall; shop (of service trades), as 飯館 restaurant	旅	lǚ　　　　* travel (M) an army brigade 旅行 travel, tour
從	cóng　　　[从] (CV) from (LC) to follow	活	huó (V) to live (SV) alive, living; lively (N) work; workmanship
興	xìng　　*　[兴] mood or desire to do sth; interest; excitement	直	zhí (直) (SV) straight, straight- 　　　forward; vertical (A) continuously
趣	qù　　　　* interest; delight	等	děng (V) to wait (for) (M) grade, class * and so on, etc.
影	yǐng　　　* shadow; reflection; image 電影 film, movie	火	huǒ (N) fire; anger (SV) angry (AT) fiery
更	gèng (A) more, still more, 　　still...-er, further	車	chē　　　　[车] (N) vehicle　(M:輛 liàng) * machine
開	kāi　　　[开] (V) to open (up/out); to start; to operate (machines, vehicles), run (a business)	過	guò　　　　[过] (V) to pass (through), to cross; to spend (time) a verb suffix
始	shǐ　　　* beginning, start 開始 (V/N) start	蘇	sū　　　*　[苏] (LC) to revive short for Suzhou, Jiangsu, Soviet and USSR　a surname
習	xí (習)　*　[习] to practise; to get accus- tomed to; habit, custom	聯	lián　　*　[联] to unite, to ally oneself with 蘇聯 Soviet Union
千	qiān (NU) thousand	舒	shū　　　* to unfold; to relax; leisurely

77

服	fú * clothes, dress (V) to yield to	清	qīng (清) (SV) clear, pure the Qing (Ch'ing) dynasty
長	cháng　　　[长] (SV) long	楚	chǔ　　　* clear, neat
算	suàn ⌐示¬ (V) to calculate, reckon, 　　compute; to regard as	必	bì　　　* must, have to; necessary 必得 must; 不必 need not
帶	dài　　　[带] (V) to bring, to take along; 　　to lead (N) belt, band, zone	歷	lì　　　*　[历] to pass through, to undergo; to experience
汽	qì (N) vapour, steam 汽車 motor car	史	shǐ (N) history a surname
票	piào (N) ticket; coupon　(M: 張)	便	biàn　　　* convenient, handy; informal; to relieve oneself: 小便 uri- nate; 大便 defecate
戲	xì　　　[戏] (N) drama, play, show 京戲 Peking opera	換	huàn (換)　　[换] (V) to change, exchange
往	wàng (CV) to, towards (LC) to go to	轉	zhuǎn　　　[转] (V) to turn; to pass on; to 　　transfer
飛	fēi　　　[飞] (V) to fly	場	chǎng　　　[场] * a place, a field (M) for performances; spell 　　of
又	yòu (A) again, then again; on 　　top of (that)	停	tíng (V) to stop, halt, pause; 　　to park, berth
些	xiē (NU/M) some, several; amount		

STROKE-ORDER

倫　亻 伫 伫 俭 俭 倫 (伦)　　[人丿]　　館　丷 全 食 飠 館 館 (馆)　　[食]

敦　亠 古 亨 亨 享 敦 敦　　[攴]　　從　彳 彴 祄 祄 祄 祄 從 (从)　[彳]

78

興　同侗侗侗侗輿興　(兴)　[臼]　　服　月肝肌服服　　　　[月]
趣　土丰走赵趄趣趣　　　[走]　　長　一「上長長長 (长) ノ上长 [長]
影　日旦昌景景影　　　　[彡]　　算　竹笪算算　　　　　[竹]
更　一一百更更　　　　　[曰]　　帶　一廿廿卅卅卅帶 (带)　[巾]
開　門門閂閂開　(开)　　[門]　　汽　氵汽汽汽　　　　　[水]
始　女如始　　　　　　　[女]　　票　一兩西覀票　　　　[示]
習　フヲヲ羽羽習習習(习)[羽]　　戲　丶丶广广庐庐虙戲戲戲[戈]
千　二千　　　　　　　　[十]　　(戏)　フ又戏戏戏
談　言訂訂談談　(谈)　　[言]　　往　彳彳彳彳往　　　　[彳]
題　日旦是是題　(题)　　[頁]　　飛　飞飞飞飞飞飛 (飞)　[飛]
旅　一亠方方扩扩旅旅　　[方]　　又　フ又　　　　　　　[又]
活　氵氵汀汗活　　　　　[水]　　些　丨卜止止此此些　　[二]
直　一十方直直　　　　　[目]　　清　氵汀沣沣清清　　　[水]
等　竹竺笙等等　　　　　[竹]　　楚　木林杢梺梺梺楚　　[木]
火　丶丷少火 丶丶丷火　　[火]　　必　丶心必必必　　　　[心]
車　一一百亘車 (车) 一七七车[車]　歷　厂厈麻歷歷歷 (历) 厂历[止]
過　冂円丹咼過　(过)　　[辶]　　史　口史史　　　　　　[口]
蘇　艹蔫蔬鮏鮇蘇　　　　[艸]　　便　亻便便便　　　　　[人]
(苏)　艹芍芳茆苏　　　　　　　　換　扌扩扩护换换换 (换)　[手]
聯　耳聑聯聯聯聯聯　　　[耳]　　轉　車軒軒軒轉 (转) 轵转转[車]
(联)　耳耵聣联联　　　　　　　　場　坦場場場 (场) 圬场　[土]
舒　人合今舍舍舒舒　　　[舌]　　停　亻停停停　　　　　[人]

VOCABULARY

倫敦 Lúndūn (PW) London

圖書館 túshūguǎn (N) library

從 cóng (CV) from (used of time and space)

興趣 xìngqù (N) interest (directed towards, not inherent in something)

　對 X 有興趣　take an interest in X

電影(兒) diànyǐng(r) (N) motion picture

更 gèng (A) still more, even more

前 qián (L) before, ago

開始 kāishǐ (V/N) start

　從....開始 starting from......

學習 xuéxí (V/N) 'learn + practise' — study

千 qiān (NU) thousand

談天(兒) tán-tiān(r) (V-O) chat, natter

問題 wèntí (N) issue, question, problem

早就 zǎojiù (A) long since

旅行 lǚxíng (V/N) travel

平常 píngcháng (SV/MA) usual, everyday, ordinary; usually

生活 shēnghuó (N/V) life; live

一直 yìzhí (A) straight through, all along, directly

法子 fázi/fǎzi (N) way, means, method

　没法子 méi fázi/fǎzi (IE) have no way of; can't be helped

等 děng (V) wait (for)　(N/M) grade, class

坐 zuò (V) sit (on)　(CV) travel by; by

火車 huǒchē (N) train

經過 jīngguò (V) pass through　(CV) by, by way of

蘇聯 Sūlián (PW) Soviet Union

舒服 shūfu (SV) comfortable

　不舒服 (SV) uncomfortable　(IE) not feel well

長 cháng (SV) long

打算 dǎsuàn (V) reckon on, have in mind to, plan to

帶 dài (V) bring, take along

小説 xiǎoshuō (N) (work of) fiction, novel

公共汽車 gōnggòng qìchē (N) 'public motor car'—— bus

票 piào (N) ticket, coupon

戲 xì (N) drama, play, show

往 wàng (CV) in direction of, towards; bound for (also pronounced wǎng)

飛機 fēijī (N) aeroplane

又 yòu (A) again, then again

　又....又.... both ....and....

(一)些 (yì)xiē (M) some, several, a small amount

國家 guójiā (N) state, country

清楚 qīngchu (SV) clear

幹麽 gànmá? (IE) do what? get up to what? what for?

必,必得 bì, bìděi (MV) must, have to

不必 bú bì no need to

歷史 lìshǐ (N) history; history book

電車 diànchē (N) tram

方便 fāngbiàn (SV) convenient

換 huàn (V) change, exchange

　換車 huàn chē (V O) change trains or buses

車站 chēzhàn (N) station, (bus) stop

過 guò (V) pass, cross

路口(兒) lùkǒu(r) (N/PW) 'road mouth' —— turning, intersection

向 xiàng (CV) toward(s)

轉 zhuǎn (V) turn

場 chǎng (M) for performances; spell of

日本 Rìběn (PW) Japan

請客 qǐng-kè (V-O) invite guest; stand treat

開 kāi (V) open (up/out); start; operate

　開車 kāi-chē (V-O) drive

停 tíng (V) stop, halt; park, berth

地鐵 dìtiě (N) short for dìxià tiědào, 'underground railway', tube

老錢在倫敦城裏的一個圖書館工作,他從小就對中國有興趣:愛看中國電影兒,愛聽中國音樂,更愛吃中國菜.幾年前開始學習中文,現在已經認識兩、三千個漢字.跟中國朋友談天兒,看普通的中文書報,都沒有甚麼大問題.他早就想到中國去旅行,看看中國人平常的生活情形,可是因為他的錢總是不夠,所以一直沒法子去.最近他覺得不能再等了,就決定坐火車經過蘇聯去北京.雖然路上得走八、九天,一定很累,一定很不舒服,可是這是去中國最便宜的法子.他朋友問他,在火車上的時間那麼長,他都打算做甚麼,是不是得帶幾十本小說看?他說他不帶小說.他不帶小說帶甚麼呢?

DIALOGUE

A: 欸,老錢!你在這兒等誰啊?

B: 等誰?!我不等誰!我等公共汽車到城裏去買票.

A: 買甚麼票?是戲票還是電影票?

B: 都不是,我去買火車票.

A: 要去旅行啊?是不是到北邊兒去?

B: 不,我往東走,到中國去.

A: 甚麼?!坐火車到中國去?那得走多少天啊?

B: 不要多少天,八、九天就夠了.

A: 從這兒到中國也有飛機啊,為甚麼不坐飛機呢?又快又舒服.

B: 誰不知道坐飛機又快又舒服,可是我的錢只夠買一張二等火車票,沒法子!

A: 坐火車都經過哪些國家啊?

B: 我還不太清楚,只知道一定要經過蘇聯.

A: 這條路真不近,在火車上的時間那麼長,你都想幹麼?恐怕得帶幾十本小說吧?

B: 不必,我只帶一本中國歷史就夠了,這條路雖然長,可是中國的歷史不是更長嗎?

(1)

A：到哪兒去啊？

B：我到西城去。

A：這麼晚了，又這麼冷，到西城去幹麼？

B：沒法子，我得去看個朋友。

A：你打算怎麼去啊？

B：我這是第一次去，不知道是坐電車好，還是坐公共汽車好。

A：你朋友家在西城甚麼地方？

B：他說就在西城圖書館後頭。

A：那我知道，坐電車去方便，一〇九路一直可以到圖書館，不用換車。

B：您知道一〇九路車站在哪兒嗎？

A：很近，從這兒往北走，過兩個路口兒，向右轉，百貨商店前頭就是。

B：多謝，多謝！

A：不謝。

(2)

A：今天星期六，晚上打算到哪兒去玩兒？

B：不想到哪兒去，你呢？

A：想去看場日本電影兒，你有沒有興趣啊？

B：你請客，我就去。

A：沒問題！你請我吃晚飯，我就請你看電影兒。

B：行！我們去吃頓日本飯怎麼樣？

A：好啊。現在就走吧，我開車。

B：城裏車那麼多，又沒地方停，還是坐地鐵去吧！

A：那太不方便了，中間兒要換車，兩頭兒還得走路。

B：你怕走路啊？大家都說走路對身體好。

A：你的身體已經夠好了，不必再走路了，還是坐我的車去吧。

SPEECH PATTERNS

(1) Coming and going

Pattern: 中國人來(英國),英國人去(中國).

1. 他今天來不來?　　他昨天說一定來.
2. 你們都去嗎?　　要是有人開車,我們就都去.
3. 他信上說甚麼?　　他說他很想來倫敦.
4. 學中文的都應該去中國嗎?　　我覺得都應該去.
5. 誰去誰那兒?　　我們這兒地方大,你們來我們這兒吧.
6. 每年來英國的外國人真不少.
   是啊,去外國的英國人也很多.
7. 他想去北京,可是沒錢,怎麼辦?　　沒法子.

(2) To and fro

Patterns: a.　　 cóng/dào 　 X 　 lái/qù

　　我 從/到 圖書館 來/去.

b.　　 cóng 　 X 　 dào 　 Y 　 lái/qù

　　他要從 法國 到 德國去.

1. 早啊,你從哪兒來?　　我從家裏來.
2. 你到哪兒去?　　我到老王那兒去.
3. 星期天不工作,沒人到這兒來嗎?　　平常很少人來.
4. 他們都想到山上去,你怎麼不去?　　山也太高,我也太胖.
5. 你們明天到青山公社,從哪兒去啊?　　我們從廠裏去.
6. 我早就想到日本去,可是一直沒機會.
7. 從湖北到廣東(去)一定得經過湖南嗎?
8. 從星期一到星期五他每天要學五十個漢字.
9. 從昨天晚上開始,外國人不准再到城外頭去了.
10. 從報上可以知道現在英國的問題很多.

(3) <u>Means of conveyance</u>

Pattern: 我每天坐公共汽車來.

1. 你們到中國去,打算怎麼去? 我們坐火車去.
2. 從倫敦到北京,坐飛機(去)得多少錢?
   普通票恐怕得一千多塊吧.
3. 老李說你要到法國去,坐火車去嗎? 不,我坐朋友的車去.
4. 從這兒到城外的東湖有電車嗎?
   沒有電車,我們得坐公共汽車去.
5. 去他們家,坐幾路車? 他們家很近,不必坐車,走路去就行了.
6. 你說我們怎麼去好?
   走路去吧,天氣這麼好,走走不是很舒服嗎?
7. 從倫敦坐火車到上海要多少天?路上得停多少站?
8. 從你家坐公共汽車到大學得多少錢? 六毛五.
9a. 你們怎麼去火車站? 我們坐地鐵去.
 b. 去火車站怎麼走?
   從這兒一直往東走,過三個路口兒,向左轉就是.

(4) <u>Purposes in coming and going</u>

Patterns: a. 我去吃飯.
          b. 我吃飯去.
          c. 我去吃飯去.

1. 你最想去甚麼地方旅行? 中國.
2. (到)哪兒去? 去城裏看戲去.
3. 他到山上去幹麼? 他去學太極拳.
4. 再喝杯茶吧? 不了,我還得到火車站去送朋友.
5. 有機會很想到中國去工作. 你是學甚麼的?
6. 這些人到我們大學來幹麼? 他們來看圖書館.
7. 他不想在生產隊了,想到山上去搞氣象去.
8. 沒事兒,請常到我們這兒來玩兒! 好,一定!

(5) <u>Question words as indefinites</u>

1. 您要買甚麼?　　a. 我想買張桌子.
　　　　　　　　　b. 我不買甚麼,看看可以嗎?

2. 今天晚上到哪兒去?　　a. 我想跟朋友去看電影兒.
　　　　　　　　　　　　b. 不到哪兒去,我想在家看看電視.

3. 他有多少中文書?　　a. 最少有五、六千本.
　　　　　　　　　　　b. 沒有多少,最多二、三十本.

4. 那些國家的生活水平怎麼樣?　　a. 很高.
　　　　　　　　　　　　　　　　b. 不怎麼高.

5. 這些問題你都清楚嗎?　　a. 很清楚.
　　　　　　　　　　　　　b. 不怎麼清楚.

6. 你對歷史小說有興趣嗎?　　a. 很有興趣.
　　　　　　　　　　　　　　b. 不怎麼有興趣. or
　　　　　　　　　　　　　　　沒甚麼興趣.

7. 你打算給誰寫信?　　a. 我打算給老李寫信.
　　　　　　　　　　　b. 我不打算給誰寫信.

8. 你甚麼地方不舒服?　　a. 我的頭不太舒服.
　　　　　　　　　　　　b. 我沒甚麼地方不舒服.

9. 西山公社有幾個工廠?　　a. 三個.
　　　　　　　　　　　　　b. 沒幾個.

　　Compare: 西山公社有幾個工廠,工人一共有三、四百.

10. 你有幾個華僑朋友?　　a. 十幾個.
　　　　　　　　　　　　　b. 沒幾個.

　　Compare: 我有幾個華僑朋友,他們只會說廣東話.

(6) <u>'Dōu' used to indicate plurality in a question</u>

1. 你都想吃甚麼?　　我想吃點兒雞,也想吃點兒魚.

2. 你們都對甚麼有興趣?
　　他們三個人對地理有興趣,我們五個人對歷史有興趣.

3. 他們都姓甚麼？　　一個姓李,一個姓錢,還有兩個姓王.
4. 明天星期天,你都想幹麼？　我想去買東西,也想去看電影兒.
5. 你帶這麼多錢,都想買甚麼啊？
　　我得買很多東西:毛衣,字典,收音機.....
6. 他們都去哪些國家？　　他們要去法國,德國,蘇聯,日本跟中國.

(7) <u>More elaborate choice-type questions</u>

```
Patterns:  a.      O....  O....  ?
                你    累    不累    ?
               這個好, 那個好  ?

            b.    shì   A   (ne),  shì   B   (ne) ?
                你  是   去  (呢), 是  不去  (呢) ?
                    是 中文難 (呢), 是 英文難 (呢) ?

            c.    shì   A   (ne),  háishì   B   (ne) ?
                你  是 喜歡  (呢), 還是 不喜歡 (呢) ?
                    是  他去  (呢), 還是  你去  (呢) ?
```

1. 你説茶好喝,咖啡好喝？　　我説咖啡好喝.
2. 是你認識的字多,還是他認識的字多？
　　我們兩個人認識的字一樣多.
3. 是他來還是你去？　　他也不來,我也不去.
4. 今天晚上吃魚好,還是吃雞好？　　我説還是吃魚好.
5. 你們怎麼去？坐火車還是坐飛機？
　　飛機票太貴,我們坐火車去.
6. 她是喜歡看電影兒呢,還是喜歡看戲？　　好像都不太喜歡.
7. 那個商店(是)在車站東邊兒,還是在車站西邊兒？
　　我也不太清楚.
8. 坐地鐵去方便,還是坐公共汽車去方便？
　　公共汽車方便:一一三路一直可以到,不必換車.
9. 是在公社搞生產容易,還是在山上搞氣象容易？
　　都不容易.
10. 是你的漢語水平高,還是她的漢語水平高？　　都不太高.

LESSON 11

晨	chén * morning	面	miàn * face; surface; side; aspect
鐘	zhōng [钟] (N) clock; large bell 十點鐘 10 o'clock 十分鐘 ten minutes	非	fēi * (LC) is not (= 不是) non-; in-; wrong short for Africa 非洲
出	chū * out (directional compl.) (V) to issue; to put up; to produce; to arise	忘	wàng (V) to forget
發	fā [发] (V) to send out; to emit; to develop; to get into a cer- tain state	馬	mǎ [马] (N) horse a surname
刻	kè * moment (M) quarter of an hour (V) to carve; to engrave	畢	bì * [毕] to finish; to accomplish; to conclude
才	cái (A) just; then and only then; not until	業	yè * [业] line of business; industry; occupation; employment; course of study
回	huí (V) to return to; to answer (M) occasion; for affairs, matters	告	gào * to tell, to inform 告訴 (V) to sue
整	zhěng * whole; complete; full; entire; to put in order ; in good order	訴	sù [诉] (V) to tell (in great de- tail); to complain; to appeal
午	wǔ * noon 中午	數	shù [数] (N) number; figure (NU) several
跑	pǎo (V) to run (to); to run about doing sth.; to run away	司	sī * to control; to be in charge of
門	mén [门] (N) door, gate; entrance; 　　gateway (M) for subjects (for study)	專	zhuān [专] (SV) concentrated; special- ized
碰	pèng (碰) (V) to touch; to bump; to meet with; to run into	計	jì [计] * to reckon, to compute (N) idea; plan; trick; stratagem

腦	nǎo '腦' [脑] (N) brain	婚	hūn * marriage 結婚 (VO) get married
懂	dǒng (V) to understand	候	hòu * time 時候 ; season; in-quire after 問候 (V) to wait (等)候
簡	jiǎn * [简] simple 簡單 ; simplified; brief	猜	cāi (猜) (V) to guess; to suspect
釋	shì * [释] to explain 解釋 ; to release; to set free	漂	piào * 漂亮 (SV) elegant; smart; beautiful; handsome
除	chú (V) to deduct; to divide (arith.) (CV) apart from	亮	liàng (SV) bright; shiny (N) light, illumination (V) to show
牛	niú (N) cattle, cow (M:頭/隻) a surname	器	qì '器' implement, untensil, ware, instrument
彈	tán [弹] (V) to pluck (a string); to flip	差	chà [差] (V) lack; differ by (SV) short of, not up to the mark
琴	qín (N) the seven-stringed lute; a general name for certain musical instruments	叔	shū/shú (N) uncle (father's younger brother)
自	zì * self; oneself 自己 ; self- (CV) from; since	爸	bà (N) pa, dad 爸爸 papa
己	jǐ * oneself; one's own	牌	pái (N) plate, tablet, placard, sign; brand; mahjong piece, dominoes, cards, etc.
結	jié [结] (V) to tie; to knot; to weave; to congeal		

Character	Stroke Order	Radical		Character	Stroke Order	Radical
晨	日 旦 尸 尽 晨 晨 晨	[日]		專	一 百 申 重 重 專	[寸]
鐘	金 釒 鋪 鐘 鐘 鐘 (钟)	[金]		(专)	二 专 专	
出	乚 屮 屮 出	[山]		計	言 計 計 (计)	[言]
發	フ ヲ ヺ ヺ゛ 㢱 癸 發 發	[癶]		腦	月 胖 胖 腦 腦 腦	[肉月]
(发)	乚 少 发 发 发			(脑)	月 扩 脑 脑 脑	
刻	亠 十 亥 亥 亥 刻	[刀刂]		懂	忄 忄 忙 懂 懂 懂	[心忄]
才	一 十 才	[手扌]		簡	⺮ 節 簡 簡 (简)	[竹]
回	冂 囗 回 回	[口]		釋	丶 丷 立 半 釆 釋 釋 釋 釋	[米]
整	ロ 車 束 敕 敕 整 整 整	[攵]		(释)	釆 釆 释 释 释	
午	ノ 一 二 午	[十]		除	阝 阝 阝 阶 阶 除 除	[阜阝]
跑	口 甲 甲 足 足 跙 趵 跑 跑	[足]		牛	ノ 一 二 牛	[牛]
門	丨 冂 冂 冋 冋 門 門 門 門	[門]		彈	弓 弓 彈 彈 彈 (弹) 弹 弹 弹	[弓]
(门)	丶 冂 门			琴	王 珏 珏 琴	[玉]
碰	石 矿 矿 矿 碰 碰 碰	[石]		自	ノ 亻 冎 自 目	[自]
面	一 丆 丙 而 面 面	[面]		己	㇎ コ 己	[己]
非	丨 丨 丬 非 非 非	[非]		結	糸 糸 紝 紝 結 (结)	[糸]
忘	丶 亠 忙 忘	[心]		婚	女 女 妒 婚 婚 婚	[女]
馬	三 丢 馬 馬 (马) 丁 马 马	[馬]		候	亻 亻 忙 忙 候 候 候	[人亻]
畢	冂 田 田 畄 畢 畢 畢	[田]		猜	ノ 犭 犭 犭 狚 猜	[犬犭]
(毕)	一 匕 比 比 比 毕			漂	氵 沪 沪 潭 漂	[水氵]
業	业 业 业 业 業 業 (业)	[木]		亮	亠 宀 古 立 亭 亮	[亠]
告	ノ 一 牛 生 告	[口]		器	吅 哭 哭 器 (器) 吅 哭 器	[口]
訴	言 訁 訴 訴 訴 (诉)	[言]		差	丷 关 羊 羊 差 (差) 兰 羊 差	[工]
數	日 昌 婁 婁 婁 數	[攵]		叔	上 未 叔	[又]
(数)	丶 丷 半 半 婁 婁 婁 数			爸	八 少 父 谷 谷 爸	[父]
司	㇆ 刁 司	[口]		牌	ノ ノ 广 片 牕 牌 牌 牌	[片]

VOCABULARY

早晨 zǎochen (TW) morning

點鐘 diǎn zhōng (M-N) hour of the clock

出發 chūfā (V) set out

刻 kè (M) quarter (of an hour)

才 cái (A) only then; not until

回來 huílai (V) come back

　回 huí (V) return to

整整 zhěngzhěng (A) fully; a whole

上午 shàngwǔ (TW) morning, a.m.

下午 xiàwǔ (TW) afternoon, p.m.

跑 pǎo (V) to run (to), (hurry) to; run away

分 fēn (M) minute (clock time)

沒想到 méi xiǎngdào (IE) unexpectedly, to one's surprise

門口(兒) ménkǒu(r) (PW) entrance

碰見 pèngjiàn (V) run into, meet

見面 jiàn-miàn (V-O) meet, see one another

非常 fēicháng (A) exceptionally

高興 gāoxìng (SV) pleased, exhilarated

忘(了) wàng(-le) (V) forget

馬上 mǎshàng (A) at once (lit. on horseback)

進 jìn (V) enter

酒館兒 jiǔguǎnr (N) pub

畢業 bì-yè (V-O) to graduate, finish school

以後 yǐhòu (TW) after, afterwards, later

告訴 gàosu (V) tell

數學 shùxué (N) mathematics

家 jiā (M) for families and business establishments

公司 gōngsī (N) company, corporation

專門 zhuānmén (SV/A) special(ly)

電子 diànzǐ (N) electron

計算機 jìsuànjī (N) calculating machine, computer

電腦 diànnǎo (N) 'electric brain'— computer

幹 gàn (V) do, work, get on with

懂 dǒng (V) understand

簡單 jiǎndān (SV) simple

解釋 jiěshì (V) explain

回 huí (M) occasion; for affairs

　一回事 yì huí shì (NU-M-N) a matter, business

怎麼一回事 zěnme yì huí shì (IE) what it's all about

小時 xiǎoshí (N/M) hour

除了....以外 chúle ....yǐwài (PH) apart from ......

最後 zuìhòu (MA) finally, eventually

只好 zhǐhǎo (A) be forced to, could only

牛 niú (N) cattle, cow

彈琴 tán qín (VO) play/strum lute

鐘頭 zhōngtóu (N) hour

腦子 nǎozi (N) brain

自己 zìjǐ (PN) oneself

結婚 jié-hūn (V-O) marry

時候 shíhou (N) time

  ...的時候 ...de shíhou (TW) when, while

好 hǎo (SV) be on good terms

分開 fēnkāi (V) separate, part

一起 yìqǐ (A) together

分鐘 fēn zhōng (M-N) minute (length of time)

聽説 tīngshuō (V/N) hear (it said) that; hearsay

猜 cāi (V) guess

漂亮 piàoliang (SV) pretty, handsome

能幹 nénggàn (SV) capable, competent

機器人 jīqìrén (N) mechanical person, robot

  機器 jīqì (N) machine, machinery

出去 chūqu (V) go out

早飯 zǎofàn (N) breakfast

差 chà (V) lack, differ by
(SV) short of, not up to the mark

  差不多 chàbuduō (SV) almost the same (lit. doesn't differ much)
(A) almost, about
(IE) not bad, just about right

叔叔 shūshu (N) uncle (father's younger brother); 'uncle' (polite usage by children)

爸(爸) bà(ba) (N) pa, dad

打牌 dǎ pái (VO) play mahjong or cards

PRESENTATION

　　昨天我到倫敦去了．早晨八點多鐘出發，晚上十一點一刻才回來，整整忙了一天．倫敦人多，車也多，到哪兒去都不容易．從上午十點到下午五點半，我一共跑了八個地方，辦了三件大事；飯也沒吃，茶也沒喝，真是又餓又累．本來打算坐六點零六分的火車回家，沒想到在車站門口兒碰見了大學同學小李．老朋友見面當然非常高興，我也忘了累，馬上就跟他進了酒館兒．每人先喝了三杯，才開始談畢業以後的情形．他告訴我他先在中學教了一年數學，又在工廠當了兩年工人，後來有人介紹他進了現在工作的這家公司，專門搞電子計算機 —— 也就是我們常說的電腦．他對這個工作非常有興趣，已經幹了六、七年了．他知道我完全不懂電腦，就用最簡單的數學跟我解釋電腦是怎麼一回事，可是他說了一個多小時，除了零跟一以外，我還是甚麼都不懂，最後我只好跟他說：

DIALOGUE

A：小李，你別'對牛彈琴'了，你說了一個多鐘頭了，我還是不懂，我們談談別的吧！

B：談別的？我搞電腦搞了這麼多年了，現在腦子裏除了電腦，甚麼都沒有了．

A：談談你自己的事吧．先告訴我結婚了沒有？

B：還沒呢！現在找個對象真不簡單，我已經找了幾年了．

A：你在大學的時候，不是有個學歷史的女朋友嗎？

B：你說的是小張吧？是，我們兩個人好了五年多，可是我進了電腦公司，她就跟我分開了．

A：為甚麼？

B：因為我總是跟電腦在一起，每天最多只能跟她見面幾分鐘．

A：那當然不行！聽說電腦也能替人找對象，是真的嗎？

B：當然是真的，電腦甚麼事都能做．有一次我問電腦，像我這樣的人應該找甚麼樣的人做對象，你猜電腦說甚麼？

A：一定說你應該找一位又漂亮、又能幹、又……

B：不對，不對，電腦說像我這樣兒的人只能找個機器人做對象！

SKETCHES

(1) A: 昨天星期天,出去了沒有?

B: 出去了.吃了早飯就到山上去了.

A: 從你家到山上得走幾個鐘頭啊?

B: 我八點十分出發,差一刻十點就到了.走了差不多一個半小時.

A: 真快啊! 天氣這麼冷,你到山上去幹麼?

B: 我去打太極拳.

A: 打太極拳一定要到山上去嗎?

B: 不一定,可是教我太極拳的老師在山上.

A: 你學了多久了?

B: 已經學了三年了.

A: 你能不能解釋解釋'太極'是怎麼一回事?

B: 要是我知道'太極'是怎麼一回事,我也到山上去了.

(2) A: 張叔叔,您來了.

B: 小胖兒,你爸爸在家嗎?

A: 我爸不在家,吃了飯就出去了.

B: 甚麼時候回來啊?

A: 恐怕得十一點吧.

B: 到哪兒去了?

A: 他沒說到哪兒去,可是我知道.

B: 可以告訴我嗎? 我有事要找他.

A: 告訴您可以,可是您不能告訴我媽.

B: 為甚麼?

A: 我爸到口兒上那家酒館兒喝酒去了,我媽最不高興我爸喝酒了.

B: 你媽也不在家嗎?

A: 不在.我媽去打牌去了.可是您別告訴我爸爸,我爸最不高興我媽打牌了.

93

(1) Time expressions

(a) Reading of clock time

1:00	一點(鐘) / 一點整
2:03	兩點(零)三分
3:10 (p.m.)	(下午) 三點十分
4:15	四點十五分 / 四點一刻
5:20 (a.m.)	(早晨) 五點二十分
6:30	六點三十分 / 六點半
7:40	七點四十分
8:45 (p.m.)	(晚上) 八點四十五分 / 八點三刻 / 差一刻九點 / 九點差一刻
9:50 (a.m.)	(上午) 九點五十分 / 差十分十點 / 十點差十分
12:55	十二點五十五分 / 差五分一點 / 一點差五分
19:47	十九點四十七分
22:30	二十二點三十分
after 2 p.m. (before 3)	下午兩點多(鐘)
5 or 6 o'clock	五、六點(鐘)
11 or 12 o'clock	十一、二點(鐘)

Pattern:　　　　Time When　V　(O)

你甚麼時候去?　　我明天上午九點去.

你每天幾點鐘吃早飯?　　八點一刻.

1. 幾點了?　　快四點了.火車四點幾分開?
2. 今天新聞甚麼時候?　　好像是九點十分.
3. 他打算甚麼時候來?　　下午兩點.
4. 你每天晚上幾點鐘睡覺?　　最早十一點半.
5. 你坐幾點(鐘)的車回來?　　我坐八點零五分的車回來.
6. 十一點五十五的火車甚麼時候到?　　差五分十二點到.

(b) Length of time in hours and minutes

1 min.	一分鐘
15 mins./1/4 hour	十五分鐘 ／ 一刻鐘
30 mins./½ hour	三十分鐘 ／ 半(個)小時 ／ 半個鐘頭
45 mins./3/4 hour	四十五分鐘 ／ 三刻鐘
55 mins.	五十五分鐘
1 hour	一(個)小時 ／ 一個鐘頭
2 hrs.	兩(個)小時 ／ 兩個鐘頭
3 hrs. 2 mins.	三小時零二分
4 1/4 hrs.	四小時十五分 ／ 四個鐘頭(零)一刻鐘
5½ hrs.	五個半小時 ／ 五個半鐘頭

Patterns: a. V Time How Long

你們要去 多 久 ?

b. V Time How Long (<u>de</u>) O

他每天看 幾個鐘頭 的 書?

or: V O, V Time How Long

他每天看書, 看 幾個鐘頭 ?

1. 做這個菜要多少分鐘?　很快, 最多五分鐘.
2. 今天的新聞長不長?　不長, 只有一刻鐘.
3. 從你家到圖書館得坐多久的車?　差不多七、八分鐘.
4. 她想學多久的中文?　最少四年.
5. 他每天教幾個小時的書?　一、三、五, 兩小時; 二、四, 三小時.
6. 你每天打多久的太極拳?　早晨三刻鐘, 晚上三刻鐘.

(2) <u>Sentence particle 'le' indicating 'accomplished fact'</u>

Patterns: a. V O <u>le ma?</u>

昨天你看電視了嗎?

b. V O (<u>le</u>) <u>méiyou?</u>

昨天你看電視了 沒有?

c. V <u>méi</u> V O ?

昨天你看沒看電視?

V <u>le</u>. or <u>Méi</u>(<u>you</u>) V.

看了. or 沒(有)看.

95

1. 早晨看報了嗎？　早晨太忙了,沒看.有甚麼新聞?
2. 星期天誰看電影兒了?　小王看了,我們都沒看.
3. 昨天你們在城裏買東西了沒有?　沒有,我們都沒帶錢.
4. 那天你也喝酒了嗎?　平常我不喝,可是那天我也喝了.
5. 你在那兒碰見誰了?　碰見老王了.
6. 昨天下午你沒寫漢字嗎?　沒有,我出去了.
7. 她已經到日本了嗎?　早就到了.
8. 去年他學中文沒有?　學了.
9. 他還沒解釋那個問題嗎?　解釋了,可是我還是不清楚.

(3) Verb-suffix '-le' for 'completed action'

(a) V-le O as a full sentence

1. 他們兩個人見面以後,沒說話就進了酒館兒.
2. 他介紹了這本新書,也解釋了電腦替人工作的問題.
3. 大家都說應該請他,所以我們就請了他.
4. 中學畢業以後,他就進了工廠.
5. 我告訴他以後,他馬上就告訴了小王.
6. 他們經過了德國,法國,最後到了英國.
7. 除了英文以外,他還學習了歷史跟地理.
8. 他弟弟十六歲就當了解放軍.

(b) Quantified object

Patterns:　a.　　　　V-le　NU M　O
　　　　　我 昨天 跑了 三個 地方.
　　　　b.　　　　V-le　Time How Long (de) O
　　　　　他 昨天 坐了 八個 鐘頭　的 飛機.
　　　　c.　　　V O,　V-le Time How Long
　　　　　他 昨天 坐飛機,坐了 八個 鐘頭.

1. 你買了幾張票?　我買了三張票.
2. 昨天晚上你寫了多少個漢字?　我一共寫了兩百四十五個.
3. 他在這兒的時候,你們吃了幾次中國飯?　三次.

4. 她去年在中國學了一點兒中文. 現在都忘了吧?

5. 我昨天只睡了四個鐘頭,今天非常累.

6. 他都去了哪些國家? 他去了法國、德國、蘇聯跟美國.

7. 中學畢業以後,他沒進大學,當了幾年售貨員.

8. 星期六你打了一天牌吧? 沒有,我只打了三個鐘頭.

9. 昨天他念了幾個鐘頭的書? 他只念了五分鐘.

10. 今天我坐了一上午的汽車. 你到哪兒去了?

11. 她在這兒一共只學了三個星期的英文.

12. 今天早晨老師沒來,我們就談了兩個鐘頭的天兒.

(c) V-le O as a dependent clause

Pattern: V -le (0), Main clause

看了朋友, 去吃飯.

1. 你甚麼時候去? 我吃了飯,馬上就去.

2. 他回去了嗎? 回去了,吃了飯就回去了.

3. 我現在可以去玩兒嗎? 不行,你得寫了字才能去玩兒.

4. 票買了嗎? 還沒呢,我打算看了老李就去買.

5. 他每天甚麼時候打太極拳? 他吃了早飯就打.

6. 你很累嗎? 不累,只是喝了酒,很想睡覺.

7. 你們甚麼時候來? 看了電影來,行不行?

8. 你給他的信寫了嗎? 寫了,昨天客人走了,我就寫了.

9. 他們結了婚,想到中國去.

10. 她學了三天,就不想學了.

11. 他們走了五分鐘,我才回來.

12. 這本數學太難了,我看了很久,還是不懂.

(4) Combination of verb-suffix '-le' and sentence particle 'le'

(a) Where the verb ends the sentence or clause, and <u>le</u> might serve a double function

1. 他來了嗎? 他早就來了.

2. 去北京的那四個人都回來了嗎?

　　兩個回來了,兩個還沒回來呢.

3. 你想吃甚麼?我給你做.　　我已經吃了,別給我做了.

4. 他們還在一起嗎?　　已經分開了.

5. 老師叫你寫的字,寫了沒有?　　還沒呢,我忘了.

6. 他請你辦的那件事,你辦了沒有?　　辦了,我已經告訴他了.

(b) Where the suffix -le is included before a simple object only if completion of the action is stressed

1. 你們都吃(了)飯了嗎?　　都吃了,一個鐘頭以前就吃了.

2. 給老王介紹個女朋友吧.

　　他已經有(了)對象了,你別替他着急了.

3. 她們怎麼還沒來?你請(了)她們了嗎?

　　請了,她們説馬上就來.

4. 他今年還不到四十歲,可是兩個女兒都進(了)大學了.

5. 十天前他就到(了)倫敦了.　　怎麼沒人告訴我啊?

6. 別看電影兒了,我請你吃飯去.

　　不行,我已經買(了)票了,不能不看.

(c) Progress up to the present

Patterns: a.　　V -le NU M (O) le

　　我喝了五杯　了,不能再喝了.

b.　　V -le Time How Long (de) O le

　　他寫了　四個多鐘頭　的漢字了,真想去睡覺.

or　　V O, V -le Time How Long le

　　他寫漢字,寫了　四個多鐘頭了,真想去睡覺.

1. 我今天已經寫了五百個字了,不能再寫了. (or:還得再寫五百.)

2. 他已經吃了五個蘋果了,還想再吃一個.

3. 他寫的那本書,你看了多少了?　　已經看了一半了.

4. 甚麼地方都沒有這種酒,我已經跑了八個酒館兒了.

5. 我問了三個人了,都說不知道那家電腦公司在哪兒.
6. 這個電影兒他已經看了三次了,你還想請他看嗎?
7. 我在這兒已經坐了三個鐘頭了,得走了.
8. 這條路真長,我走了一個多小時了,才走了一半.
9. 他在這個單位已經幹了二十五年了,很想到別的單位去.
10. 王先生教書教了十八年了,他自己也不知道一共教了多少學生.
11. 我們已經學了十個星期的中文了,有人還想學,有人已經不想學了.

(5) Where verb-suffix '-le' is not used

1. 以前他每年都要到中國去(X)三次. (habitual activity)
   Contrast: 他去年到中國去了三次.
2. 去年他們找(X)我教了三個星期的外語. (pivotal construction)
3. 那天他去(X)城裏買了不少東西. (verbal expressions in series)
4. 我早晨去看(X)他的時候,他說(X):"要是你昨天來....."
   (direct speech)
5. 我早晨去看(X)他的時候,他說(X)要是我昨天去.....
   (indirect speech)
6. 昨天他覺得(X)不太舒服,今天已經好了. (dispositional verb)
7. 我們昨天決定(X)明天早晨出發. (verbal construction as object)

(6) Specific relative time

Patterns: a. ...yǐqián (before, ago)　　三年以前,沒人知道這個名字.
　　　　　 b. ...de shíhou (while, when)　他來的時候,我們都不在家.
　　　　　 c. ...yǐhòu (after)　　　　　解放以後,他就到了我們單位.

1. 到中國去以前,最好學點兒中文.
2. 他每天晚上睡覺以前,都要看半個鐘頭的小說.
3. 三個星期以前,我在朋友家認識了一位專門搞電腦的華僑.

4. 你們做中國菜的時候,別忘了告訴我.

5. 沒事的時候,他就喜歡彈琴.

6. 四年以後你們都能畢業嗎? 畢業以後打算幹甚麼呢?

7. 這個問題經過他解釋以後,我們都很清楚了.

8. 見面以後我才知道她那麼難看,真沒想到.

9. 這個菜太好吃了! 沒吃以前想吃,吃了以後更想吃!

10. 結婚以前她說甚麼他都說行,結婚以後她說甚麼他都說不行.

(7) <u>Inclusiveness and exclusiveness (with question words as indefinites)</u>

Pattern: 你想吃甚麼?　a. 我甚麼都想吃.
　　　　　　　　　　　　b. 我甚麼都/也不想吃.

1. 他要買甚麼?　　a. 他甚麼都要買.　b. 他甚麼都不要買.

2. 誰認識這個人?　　a. 誰都認識.　b. 誰都不認識.

3. 你想到哪兒去旅行?　a. 我哪兒都想去.　b. 哪兒都可以.
　　　　　　　　　　　　c. 除了中國,我哪兒也不想去.

4. 他說我們哪天可以出發?　a. 他說哪天都行.
　　　　　　　　　　　　　b. 他說哪天都不行,他不准我們去.

5. 昨天晚上你做甚麼了?　a. 我沒做甚麼,看了兩個鐘頭的電視.
　　　　　　　　　　　　b. 甚麼都沒做,看了兩個鐘頭的電視.

6. 電腦能替人做甚麼?
　　除了不能替人吃飯睡覺以外,甚麼都能做.

7. 她會做魚嗎?　a. 會,她怎麼做都好吃.
　　　　　　　　b. 不會,她怎麼做都不好吃.

8. 你懂了嗎?　　這個問題太難了,他怎麼解釋我都不懂.

(8) <u>'Jiù' and 'cái' contrasted</u>
<u>(note that 'cái' does not normally combine with 'le')</u>

1a. 他九點鐘就來了,太早了.

b. 他十點半才來,太晚了.

100

2a. 他說行就行.

b. 他說行才行.

3a. 我們人少,三瓶差不多就夠了.

b. 我們人多,三十瓶才夠.

4a. 這條路很近,我們走了十分鐘就到了.

b. 這條路不近,我們走了四十分鐘才到.

5a. 見面以前,我就猜她很漂亮.

b. 見面以後,我才知道她很漂亮.

6a. 我們到了那兒,不到一分鐘他就來了.

b. 我們到了那兒,等了一刻鐘他才來.

7a. 這件事很簡單,他就能辦. (他不太能幹.)

b. 這件事很不簡單,她才能辦. (她非常能幹.)

8a. 他吃了半碗就飽了.

b. 他吃了五碗還不飽.

c. 他吃了八碗才飽.

9a. 老李還沒走吧?　　走了,昨天就走了.

b. 老李已經走了吧?　　還沒呢,他明天才走.

(9) 'Yǐjing ... le' versus 'hái bù/méi ... ne'

1. 你們都懂了吧?　　他們已經懂了,我的腦子不行,還不懂呢.

2. 這些機器你們都會用了嗎?
　簡單的已經會了,難的還不太會呢.

3. 你們都吃了嗎?　　他們三個已經吃了,我們兩個還沒吃呢.

4. 客人都來了嗎?　　男的都已經來了,女的都還沒來呢.

5. 他們六個人去了沒有?
　三個已經到了,兩個在路上,一個還沒出發呢.

6. 他們都回來了嗎?
　去北京的早就回來了,去上海的還沒回來呢.

7. 你給家裏的信都寫了嗎?
　給父親的已經寫了,給叔叔的還沒寫呢.

101

8. 這四個姐妹都結婚了嗎?
   老大、老三、已經結了;老二、老四、還沒呢.

(10) 'Chúle ... (yǐwài)', apart from

1. 除了數學,他對甚麼都沒興趣.
2. 他說的中國話,除了他自己以外沒人懂.
3. 除了學習中文以外,我們還得學習中國歷史.
4. 他除了喝酒以外,也喜歡打牌.
5. 除了賣房子以外,沒有別的法子嗎?

附	fù * to be attached, added, enclosed	望	wàng * [望] to look towards; (to) hope
園	yuán * [园] garden 公園 park; 果園 orchard	將	jiāng '將' [将] (LC) to take (A) to be about to 將来 (in the) future
片	piàn (M) stretch, expanse; slice, thin piece	月	yuè * moon 月亮 (N/M) month 三 月 March; 三個月 3 months
林	lín * woods, grove (樹) 林子 a surname	課	kè [课] (N) subject; course; class (M) lesson
治	zhì * to govern; to manage; to control (V) to heal, treat	錄	lù [录] (V) to record, to tape-record * record; register
醫	yī [医] (N) medical science (V) to give medical treatment	休	xiū * to cease; to rest
院	yuàn * court; institution 院子 courtyard 醫院 hospital; 學院 college	息	xī, xí * to rest 休息 ; to cease breathe
大	dài * 大夫 (medical) doctor	復	fù * [复] again, anew; to recover; to review/revise (lessons)復習
流	liú (V) to flow	心	xīn (N) heart; mind; feeling; intention; centre, core
練	liàn [练] (V) to drill, to practise	班	bān (N/M) class (of students); schedule of bus, train or plane; shift of work
功	gōng (N) merit; achievement; skill 功夫 'kung fu'	正	zhèng (SV) right, upright, obverse (A) just right; to be on the point of ....-ing 正要
希	xī * rare; infrequent; to hope	忽	hū * suddenly 忽然 ; to neglect

103

剛	gāng [刚] * hard, strong (A) just; only just 剛才 just now, a moment ago	州	zhōu (N/M) old administrative 　　　region 廣州 Guangzhou Canton City
校	xiào * school, college	住	zhù (V) to live (at), to reside * to stop
食	shí * food (LC) to eat	船	chuán (N) boat, ship (M:隻)
堂	táng * hall (M) for teaching period	句	jù * sentence (M) for words, sentences, 　　lines of verse
戴	dài (V) to wear, to put on (hat, gloves, trappings, glasses, etc.) a surname	運	yùn [运] (V) to move about; to trans- 　　　port 運氣 (good) luck
錶	biǎo [表] (N) watch (M:塊/隻)	騎	qí [骑] (V) to ride; to sit on the 　　back of
概	gài (槪) * [概] in general, approximate 大概 general idea; on the whole; probably	借	jiè (V) to borrow; to lend 借給
號	hào * [号] (ordinal) number; day of month; date; name; mark 一月四號 Jan. 4	輛	liàng [辆] (M) for vehicles

STROKE-ORDER

附	阝阿阿阡一附附 [阜阝]	流	氵汸法流 [水氵]
圓	门冋冏周周围围圓 (园)[囗]	練	糸糿綀綀綵練 [糸]
片	丿丿广片 [片]	(练)	纟纟纰练练
林	木林 [木]	功	工丂功 [力]
治	氵汻治 [水氵]	希	丿乂兰关希希 [巾]
醫	一医医医医医醫醫 (医)[酉]	望	亠亠切钥望望望 (望)[月]
院	阝广陀陀院 [阜阝]	將	㇄丬丬丬爿爿将将将 [寸]
大	一ナ大 [大]	(将)	丬丬丬丬将

104

月 丿 丿 月 月　　　　　　　　　　　[月]　　　堂 丶 小 山 尚 堂　　　　　　　　[土]

課 言 訂 課 課 (课)　　　　　　　[言]　　　戴 士 查 声 查 壹 轰 戴 戴 戴　[戈]

錄 金 釒 釸 鉾 鋊 錄　　　　　　[金]　　　錶 金 釒 鋔 鈺 鍀 銇 錶 錶 (表)　[金]

(录) ⁊ ⁊ ヨ 寻 寻 录　　　　　　　　　概 木 柏 栒 槵 槩 概　　　　　　[木]

休 亻 休　　　　　　　　　　　　　[人]　　(概) 木 木 柝 柝 柅 根 概

息 自 息　　　　　　　　　　　　[心]　　　號 口 므 号 号 号 驴 驴 號 (号)　[虍]

復 彳 彳 狆 狆 復 復 (复)　　　[彳]　　　州 丶 丿 小 州 州 州　　　　　　[巛]

心 丶 心 心 心　　　　　　　　　[心]　　　住 亻 亻 仁 住 住　　　　　　　[人]

班 王 玉 玎 班　　　　　　　　　[玉]　　　船 丿 介 舟 身 船 船　　　　　　[舟]

正 一 丁 下 正 正　　　　　　　[止]　　　句 丿 勹 句　　　　　　　　　　[口]

忽 丿 勹 勿 忽　　　　　　　　　[心]　　　運 一 宣 軍 運 (运) 二 云 运　[辶]

剛 冂 冂 門 冏 岡 岡 剛 (刚)　[刀]　　　騎 馬 駼 騎 騎 騎 (骑)　　　　　[馬]

校 木 朴 杙 柼 柼 校　　　　　[木]　　　借 亻 亻 仁 仲 佳 借　　　　　　[人]

食 人 人 今 今 令 令 食 食 食　[食]　　　輛 車 斬 斬 軿 輛 (辆)　　　　　[車]

VOCABULARY

過 guò (V) pass, cross, go through
(V suffix) 'experiential'
suffix

別人 biéren (N) other people, others

附近 fùjìn (PW) vicinity, near by

醫院 yīyuàn (N/PW) hospital

公園(兒) gōngyuán(r) (N/PW) park,
public gardens

有名 yǒu-míng (SV) famous

片 piàn (M) stretch, expanse; slice,
thin piece

大夫 dàifu (N) medical doctor

樹林子 shùlínzi (N) woods, grove

上 (大,中,小) 學 shàng (dà-,zhōng-,xiǎo-)
xué (VO) attend school

中午 zhōngwǔ (TW) noon

從來 cónglái (A) (t)hitherto, up till
now/then

看到 kàndào (V) see, catch sight
of

從來不V　　never

東方 dōngfāng (PW) orient(al)

從來沒V過　　never

一邊兒...一邊兒... yìbiānr...
yìbiānr...(C)
on the one hand... on the other
hand...(reducible to biān...biān..
with monosyllabic verbs)

不過 búguò (C) however, nevertheless

流利 liúlì (SV) fluent

練 liàn (V) practise, train (in)

三明治 sānmíngzhì (N) sandwich

功夫 gōngfu (N) skill, art, 'kung fu';
labour, effort

希望 xīwàng (V/N) hope

将来 jiānglái (TW) in future

前年 qiánnián (TW) year before last

月 yuè (N) month

一月,二月...yī yuè, èr yuè, etc. (TW) January, February, etc.

又 yòu (A) then again; (do sth.) further; go on to (do sth.); on top of that

課 kè (M) lesson

錄 lù (V) record

錄音 lù-yīn (V-O) 'record sound'; (make a) recording

練習 liànxí (V) practise, drill (N) exercise, practice

休息 xiūxi (V) rest, take a break

復習 fùxí (V) revise (N) revision

用功 yònggōng (SV) diligent, industrious (in one's studies)

心 xīn (N) heart; mind

上星期五 shàng xīngqī-wǔ (TW) last Friday

班 bān (N/M) shift, duty; class (of students)

下班 xià bān (VO) come off duty

正 zhèng (SV/A) straight, right; just, precisely

正要 zhèngyào (A) just about to

忽然 hūrán (MA) suddenly

午飯 wǔfàn (N) lunch

請 qǐng (polite) (IE) please (go ahead, indulge)

剛才 gāngcái (TW) just now, a moment ago

學校 xuéxiào (N) school, college

食堂 shítáng (N) refectory, canteen

戴 dài (V) wear, put on (hat, gloves, trappings, etc.)

錶 biǎo (N) watch

大概 dàgài (MA) probably; in general

進來 jìnlai (V) come in

鐘 zhōng (N) clock

一會兒 yíhuìr (TW) a short while (also yìhuǐr)

上課 shàng kè (VO) start class; attend class

飯館兒 fànguǎnr (N)
館子 guǎnzi (N) } restaurant

下館子 xià guǎnzi (VO) go to a restaurant

上(個)月 shàng (ge) yuè (TW) last month

號 hào (N) number; day of month

廣州 Guǎngzhōu (PW) Canton City

來信 lái xìn (VO) send ('make come') a letter; incoming letter

住 zhù (V) live, stay, reside

下(個)月 xià (ge) yuè (TW) next month

學生 xuésheng (N) student, pupil

船 chuán (N) boat, ship

北方人 běifāng rén (N) northerner

辦法 bànfǎ (N) way, means, method

句 jù (M) for words, sentences

運氣 yùnqi (N) luck (good or bad)

騎 qí (V) ride

自行車 zìxíngchē (N) bicycle

剛 gāng (A) just, only just

飛 fēi (V) fly

借 jiè (V) borrow, lend

輛 liàng (M) for vehicles

北海公園 Běihǎi Gōngyuán (PW) (north lake) park in Peking

106

PRESENTATION

你去過大學附近的那個公園兒嗎?裏頭除了有一片樹林子以外,還有一個小湖.去過的人都說那兒的風景不錯.中午天氣好的時候,我們常常看到一位東方人坐在湖邊兒的椅子上,一邊兒看書,一邊兒吃三明治.這位先生不是別人,他就是大學醫院很有名的王大夫.王大夫的父母都是中國人,可是他是在英國生的.小學、中學、大學也都是在英國上的,從來沒到過中國.不過他能說很流利的廣東話,也練過幾種功夫,那都是小時候他父親教他的.他很希望將來有機會到中國去工作,所以前年九月又開始學習普通話,到現在已經學了快兩年了.他沒有中文老師,是自己學的.一個星期最少學一課.每天早晨聽錄音,晚上練習漢字.中午休息的時候還要到湖邊兒去復習.非常用功,好像他一天不學中文,心裏就不舒服.上星期五中午下班以後他買了兩塊三明治,又到了湖邊兒,正要開始邊吃邊看的時候,忽然後頭有人叫他:

DIALOGUE

A: 王大夫,您好啊!這兒風景真不錯!

B: 欸!小李,是你啊,吃午飯了嗎?我這兒有三明治.

A: 您請吧,我吃了,剛才在學校食堂吃的.嗯,對不起,請問您現在幾點了?我沒戴錶.

B: 現在是......欸?我的錶大概忘在醫院了,不過我剛才進來的時候,門口的大鐘還不到一點半.

A: 那好,我還可以再休息一會兒,我們兩點才上課呢.王大夫,您好像很久沒到我們飯館兒來了,天天吃三明治怎麼行啊?

B: 最近太忙了,已經有兩、三個月沒下過館子了.家裏人都好吧?

A：都好.我父親回中國去了,您知道嗎?

B：我沒聽說啊,是甚麼時候走的?要去多久啊?

A：他是上月二十三號上的飛機,二十五號晚上到的廣州,現在住在我叔叔家.昨天來信說恐怕下個月才能回來.

B：他以前回去過嗎?

A：三十年前他做學生的時候回去過一次,那次是坐船回去的,在路上整整走了一個月.

B：欸,小李,你不是在英國生的嗎?怎麼能說這麼流利的普通話?在哪兒學的?

A：我們從小在家就說普通話.我媽是北方人,不會說廣東話,也沒學過英文,所以我們都跟她說普通話.

B：你們真好!現在很多華僑家裏都說英文,忘了自己是從哪兒來的.你想想:中國人不會說中國話怎麼行啊?

A：我們開始上小學以後,也常常在家裏說英文,可是我母親想了一個好辦法,叫我們一定得說中國話.

B：甚麼好辦法?

A：很簡單:誰說中國話她就給誰吃中國飯;誰說英文她就給誰吃三明治.我們都怕吃三明治,所以現在才都能說幾句中國話.

B：你們運氣真好.我現在天天練習說中國話,可是還得在這兒吃三明治!

(1) A：你見過我的朋友李大明嗎？

B：沒見過,不過好像聽你説過這個人.

A：有機會我可以給你們介紹介紹.這個人你應該認識認識.

B：為甚麽?

A：這個人非常不簡單:他來英國以前在中國學過數學,辦過工廠,搞過新聞,還寫過三本小説.

B：真的嗎?到英國以後他做過甚麽事?

A：他進過工廠,當過售貨員,學過歷史,教過太極拳,去年又開始搞電腦.....

B：這個人真行,我從來沒聽説過有這麽能幹的人.他現在在哪兒工作啊?

A：進了醫院了.

B：噢,當了大夫了?

A：不是,不是.大夫説他的腦子得休息休息!

(2) A：剛才騎自行車來的那個中國學生是誰?

B：他姓牛,剛從上海來的,現在就住在我那兒.

A：你是在哪兒認識他的?

B：我們是前年在北京認識的。

A：我不知道你最近回過中國,一個人去的嗎?

B：不是,我是跟兩個朋友一起去的。

A：從這兒到北京你們飛了多少個小時?

B：我們不是坐飛機去的,飛機票太貴了,我們是坐火車去的。

A：你們在北京都看了些甚麽地方啊?

B：太多了.我們三個人借了三輛自行車,天天騎車出去玩兒,那些有名的地方我們差不多都去了。

A：真的?能不能説説給我們聽聽?

B：沒問題,可是不知道你們有沒有時間,因為只説北海公園恐怕我就得説一晚上。

SPEECH PATTERNS

(1) <u>Verbal suffix '-guo' as a sign for the indefinite past</u>

Patterns: a.   V -<u>guo</u> O   <u>ma</u>?

你 坐 過 飛機 嗎 ?

b.   V -<u>guo</u> O   <u>méiyou</u>?   V -<u>guo</u>./ Méi V -<u>guo</u>.

你 坐 過 飛機 沒有 ?   坐 過./ 沒 坐 過.

c.   V (-<u>guo</u>) <u>méi</u>(you) V -<u>guo</u> O ?

你 坐 (過) 沒 (有) 坐 過飛機 ?

1. 你吃過中國飯沒有?   吃過,我常吃.

2. 你去過廣州嗎?   去過,小時候跟父母去過一次.

3. 您以前來過倫敦嗎?   沒來過這是第一次.

4. 你聽説過這種電腦嗎?   聽説過,我們公司用的就是這種.

5. 這本小説你沒看過嗎?   沒看過,我不太喜歡看歷史小説.

6. 他練過多久的功夫?   一共練過八個月.

7. 你從來不看中國電影嗎?

很少看.在中國二十年,我只看過一回.

8. 你好像從來沒喝過這麽多酒.

是啊,因為我從來沒這麽高興過.

9. 最近你們那兒天氣怎麽樣?   上星期冷過兩天,這星期不錯.

10. 她一直這麽瘦嗎?   是啊.她從來沒胖過.

11a. 最近我去看過她兩次.

  b. 最近我看過兩次中國電影.

(2) <u>Verb '-le' and verb '-guo' contrasted</u>

1a. 老李去不去? <u>他以前去過</u>.不想再去了.

 b. 老王去不去? <u>他已經去了</u>.

2a. <u>他到中國去過</u>,知道一點兒中國的情形.

 b. <u>他到中國去了</u>,大概下月十五號才能回來.

3a. <u>他當過解放軍</u>,現在是公社幹部.

 b. <u>他當了解放軍</u>,身體更好了.

4a. 沒想到他碰見了這種事，你說怎麼辦？
 b. 老李碰見過這種事，他知道應該怎麼辦。
5a. 我買過一本他寫的小說，現在不知道到哪兒去了。
 b. 我買了一本他寫的小說，打算在船上看。
6a. 他沒喝過中國茶，當然不知道中國茶怎麼樣。
 b. 昨天他沒喝中國茶，只喝了一杯咖啡。

(3) 'Zai' used as verb complement

Pattern:　　　　V<u>zai</u>　　O
　　　　　　您 住 在 哪兒？　　我 住 在 倫敦。

1. 那邊兒人多，我們就坐在這兒休息休息吧。
2. 我們怎麼走？
　　你別怕，我走在你前頭，他跟在你後頭，你走在中間兒，行不行？
3. 很多沒有家的人晚上睡在火車站。
4. 他們兩個人坐在公園兒的椅子上，又吃又喝。
5. 別人都有書，你怎麼沒書？　　我也有，可是忘在家裏了。
6. 小孩子坐汽車的時候，都喜歡坐在前頭。
7. 你看我這個東西戴在這兒好不好看？　　戴在哪兒都不好看。
8. 他(是)哪兒人？　　他生在北京，可是小學、中學都是在上海念的。
9. 名字寫在甚麼地方？　　就寫在裏頭吧。
10. 他們五個人住在一起，三個住在前頭，兩個住在後頭。
11. 你的時間應該用在聽錄音上，不應該用在聽音樂上。
12. 他們兩個人走在樹林子裏，一邊兒談天兒，一邊兒看風景。
13. 生活在今天的英國，你覺得有希望嗎？
14. 那天運氣真不好，我在路上走，忽然一個東西打在我的頭上....

(4) Place as adverbial compared with place as complement
(∼ = similar to,　≠ = distinct from)

1a. 您住在哪兒？ ∼　b. 您在哪兒住？
2a. 我們坐在外邊兒吧。 ∼　b. 我們在外邊兒坐吧。

3a. 他天天睡在公園兒裏. ～ b. 他天天在公園兒裏睡.

4a. 請你寫在桌子上. ≠ b. 請你在桌子上寫.

5a. 錶不能戴在這兒. ≠ b. 在這兒不能戴錶.

6a. 錄在哪兒? ≠ b. 在哪兒錄?

(5) 'Shi ... de' construction to bring out attendant circumstances

(a) Without object

Patterns: a.   (shi)   Time   V   de
　　　　　 他　是　甚麼時候　來　的?　　是上個月來的.

        b.   (shi)   Place   V   de
　　　　　 他　是　從　哪兒　來　的?　　是從中國來的.

        c.   (shi)   Means   V   de
　　　　　 他　是　　怎麼　　來　的?　　是坐飛機來的.

1. 你叔叔是甚麼時候走的?　　是上星期三走的.

2. 你不是去年九月來的嗎?　　不是,我是去年八月來的.

3. 這些人都是從蘇聯來的嗎?
　　一半是從蘇聯來的,一半是從東德來的. (東德, 'East Germany')

4. 他是不是在英國生的?
　　不是,不過小學、中學都是在英國上的.

5. 你這件毛衣真漂亮,在哪兒買的?
　　不漂亮,就是在我家附近的那個商店買的.

6. 你們是在哪兒碰見的?　　在北京車站門口兒,沒想到吧.

7. 今天你們是怎麼來的?　　他們是走路來的,我是騎車來的.

8. 老王是怎麼去的?　　他是坐船去的.

9. 你是不是跟他一起來的?　　不是,我是自己一個人來的.

10. 她是一九七幾年畢業的?　　她是七七年畢業的.

(b) With object

Patterns: a.   (shi)   Time   V   O(PN) de
　　　　　 他　是　甚麼時候　去找你　的?　　上星期六早晨.

        b.   (shi) Place   V   de   O
　　　　　 你　是　在哪兒　吃的　午飯?　　在學生食堂吃的.

1. 你是去年幾月碰見他的?

好像是六月,就在北海公園兒門口兒.

2. 你是在哪兒認識她的? 我們是在公安局認識的.

3. 他是哪天給你的錢? 忘了,不是星期六就是星期五.

4. 你是甚麼時候買的票?
   昨天下班以後買的,是跟朋友借的錢.

5. 你叔叔是哪年去的美國? 就是我生的那年.

6. 他們是幾月幾號結的婚? 六月十五號.

7. 你們是不是昨天做的練習? 不是,我們是上星期四做的.

8. 你是在哪兒買的自行車?
   就在我們工廠附近的那家百貨公司.

9. 你今天幾點鐘聽的錄音?
   中午十二點聽的,整整聽了一個鐘頭.

10. 你們是怎麼去的醫院? 坐朋友的車去的.

11. 是誰說的我的中文沒希望了? 是別人說的,不是我.

12. 是誰告訴你的他從來不抽烟? 是他自己告訴我的.

13a. 我下午沒出去,我(是)早晨買的菜.

  b. 你看,這就是我早晨買的菜.

14. 他是昨天來的. ≠ 他(就)是昨天來的(那個)人.

(6) Verb'-le'/verb'-guo' contrasted with 'shi ... de'

1a. 我去過海德公園. ('Hyde Park')

 b. 你是甚麼時候去的?

2a. 老李到法國去了.

 b. 他是怎麼去的?

3a. 老王已經坐船走了.

 b. 他是在哪兒上的船?

4a. 他們已經結婚了.

 b. 是幾月結的?在哪兒結的?

5a. 我昨天買了一個小鐘.

 b. 你是跟誰一起去買的?

113

6a. 她以前學過三年中文.

 b. 她是用甚麼法子學的?

7a. 他上過大學.

 b. 他是哪年畢業的?

8a. 昨天我做了兩百塊三明治.

 b. 你是替誰做的?

(7) <u>Time elapsed and time within which</u>

Patterns: a. 他一天聽半小時的錄音.

 b. 他一天沒聽錄音.

1. 他一個星期不學漢字,就不舒服.
   cf.他一個星期學兩百個漢字.

2. 她一個星期沒學漢字. cf.她一個星期學了兩百個漢字.

3. 去年他差不多(有)三個月沒工作. cf.去年他工作了三個月.

4. 我已經(有)十年沒說法文了,完全都忘了.

5. 我很久沒給他寫信了,不知道他最近怎麼樣.

6. 買了汽車以後,他已經(有)兩年沒騎自行車了.

7. 她去年在中國,三個月沒說過半句英文.

8. 他已經三天沒喝酒了,當然沒有甚麼精神了.

9a. 她練習了兩年.

 b. 她沒練習兩年,只練習了一年半.

 c. 她兩年沒練習了.

10a. 他坐了三天的汽車.

 b. 他沒坐三天(的汽車),只坐了兩天.

 c. 他三天沒坐汽車.

(8) <u>Verbs of locomotion</u>

1. 上山/下山　　上山容易,下山難.

2. 上車 / 下車　　你是在哪兒上的車?打算在哪站下車?

3. 上飛機 / 下飛機　　這些人是要上飛機的;那些人是剛下飛機的.

4. 上哪兒?　　他上哪兒了?

5. 上館子 or 下館子　　他們有錢,常常下館子.

6. 上學　　孩子們早晨七點上學.

   他才四歲,還沒上學呢.

   他將來希望到外國去上大學.

7. 上課 / 下課　　我們學校九點鐘開始上課.

   　　　　　　時間到了,老師忘了下課.

8. 進城 / 出城　　早晨進城的人多,晚上出城的人多.

9. 回家　　下了課,我得馬上騎車回家.

(9) Verbs of motion compounded with 'lai' and 'qu'

1. 進來　　外頭那麼冷,你為甚麼不進來?
   進去　　裏頭人太多,我不想進去。

2. 出來　　你出來看看,外頭真漂亮.
   出去　　你出去看看,外頭好像有人說話.

3. 回來　　已經十二點了,他怎麼還沒回來,我不等他了.
   回去　　已經十二點了,我得回去了,再見!

4. 上來　　山上風景真好,你們都上來吧.
   上去　　我太累了,我不上去,我在這兒等你們.

5. 下來　　山上太冷了,你們下來吧.
   下去　　你們先下去,我馬上就來.

6. 買來　　菜已經買來了.
   買去　　他買去的書都是沒人要的.

7. 送來　　電視機已經買了,明天送來.(電視機,'T.V. set')
   送去　　他要看這本書,你給他送去好吧?

8. 過來　　請你過來看看這是甚麼.
   過去　　請你過去跟他們說,請他們過來談談.

樓	lóu [楼] (N) storied building 三樓 3rd floor (British second)	慢	màn (SV) slow
婦	fù * [妇] woman 婦女 women (as a class)	連	lián [连] (V) to join (CV) even (including) 連… 也/都
兄	xiōng * elder brother	較	jiào [较] * to compare (A) comparatively; fairly; quite
倆	liǎ [俩] (NU+M) two (fusion of 兩 and 個)	了	liǎo (V) to finish; to conclude 不得了 (SV) awful, terrible (SV comp) awfully
臉	liǎn [脸] (N) face	唱	chàng (V) to sing
眼	yǎn (N) eye 眼睛 (M: 隻 & 雙)	歌	gē (N) song (LC) to sing 國歌 national anthem
睛	jīng * eyeball	離	lí [离] (V) to leave (a place) (CV) (distant) from
長	zhǎng [长] (V) to grow * elder; senior; head; chief 校長 headmaster, principal	好	hào (V) to be fond of, to be fond of …-ing
比	bǐ (V) to compare (CV) compared with short for Belgium 比利時	奇	qí (SV) peculiar; rare; won- derful
雙	shuāng 隻 [双] (M) pair of, couple of *two; twin; dual; double	各	gè (SP) each; various
聰	cōng * [聪] (LC) faculty of hearing; acute (of hearing) 聰明 intelligent, clever	怪	guài (SV) strange; odd; queer (V) to blame
性	xìng * * quality; nature; character (N) sex 男/女性 the male/female sex	答	dá (V) to answer, to reply 回答 (V/N) answer, reply

雨	yǔ (N) rain 下雨 (V-O) to rain	關	guān '關' [关] (V) to shut, close; to turn off (N) pass; barrier
窗	chuāng (N) window 窗户／窗子	係	xì　　　* [系] (LC) is; is of the nature of 關係 relation(ship); relevance
戶	hù * door (M) a household	木	mù　　　* wood, trees (AT) wooden
糊	hú　　　* paste; to stick with paste	意	yì　　　* idea; meaning 意思; intention 有(沒)意思 be (un)interesting
塗	tú [涂] (V) to spread; to smear; to scribble 糊塗 muddled; confused	思	sī　　　* to think; to long for 思想 thought, thinking
麻	má (N) hemp (SV) numb; insensitive	白	bái (SV) white; plain; fair, pale (of complexion)
煩	fán [烦] (SV) be vexed; be annoyed (V) to bother 麻煩 trouble; troublesome	嘴	zuǐ [嘴] (N) mouth　　　(M:張)
記	jì [记] (V) to memorize, to remember, to record (N) mark; sign	笨	bèn (SV) stupid; obtuse; clumsy
首	shǒu * head; beginning; first (M) for songs and poems		

STROKE-ORDER

樓	木 柏 楎 椲 樓 樓 樓	[木]	眼	｜ ｜｜ 目 目 目 目 眼 眼 眼	[目]
(楼)	木 术 杓 杓 杅 杵 楼 楼		睛	目 目 睦 睛	[目]
婦	女 女 女 女 婦 婦 (妇)	[女]	長	一 「 F 耳 長 長 長 (长) 二 长	[長]
兄	口 尸 兄	[儿]	比	一 上 比 比	[比]
倆	亻 行 倆 倆 倆 (俩)	[人]	雙	隹 雔 雙 (双) 又 双	[隹]
臉	月 胪 胗 脸 臉 (脸)	[肉月]	聰	耳 聊 聊 聰 聰 (聪)	[耳]

117

性	忄 性	[心]
慢	忄 忄 幔 慢	[心]
連	豆 車 連 (连)　一 七 卋 车 连	[辶]
較	車 軒 軒 軒 較 (较)	[車]
了	了 了	[｜]
唱	口 唱 唱	[口]
歌	哥 哥 哥 歌 歌	[欠]
離	亠 卋 卋 离 离 离 離 (离)	[佳]
好	女 好	[女]
奇	大 奇	[大]
各	夕 夕 夂 各	[口]
怪	忄 怪 怪	[心]
答	竹 笁 答	[竹]
雨	一 雨 雨 雨 雨	[雨]
窗	宀 穴 宛 窗 窗	[穴]

户	丶 宀 二 户	[户]
糊	丷 丷 半 半 粘 糊	[米]
塗	氵 沪 涂 塗 (涂)	[土]
麻	广 床 麻	[麻]
煩	火 煩 (烦)	[火]
記	言 訂 記 (记)	[言]
首	丷 丷 艹 芦 首 首	[首]
關	門 閂 閂 閂 閂 開 關 關 (关)	[門]
係	亻 伫 仔 係 係 (系)	[人]
木	一 十 木	[木]
意	亠 立 音 意	[心]
思	田 思	[心]
白	丿 竹 臼 白	[曰]
嘴	口 叮 叮 叮 叮 叮 啃 嘴 (嘴)	[口]
笨	竹 笁 竻 笨	[竹]

VOCABULARY

樓 lóu (N) storied building
　　(M) floor
　三樓 sān lóu (PW) 3rd floor (British second)
　樓上 lóu-shàng (PW) upstairs
　樓下 lóu-xià (PW) downstairs
夫婦 fūfù (N) husband and wife, married couple
兄弟 xiōngdì (N) brothers; younger brother
倆 liǎ (N+M) two (= liǎng ge)
臉 liǎn (N) face
眼睛 yǎnjing (N) eye
長 zhǎng (V) grow
得 de (K) complement marker
　長得 zhǎng de (grow to) be — (descriptive of physical characteristics)

像 xiàng (SV) be alike
極了 -jíle (SV comp) extremely
比 bǐ (V) compare
　　(CV) compared with
以為 yǐwéi (V) think that, have the idea that, assume (wrongly)
雙生 shuāngshēng (N) twins
　雙生兄弟 shuāngshēng xiōngdì (N) twin brothers
聰明 cōngming (SV) intelligent, bright, clever
可愛 kě'ài (SV) lovable, likable, lovely
性情 xìngqing (N) nature, temperament
不同 bù-tóng (SV) dissimilar, different

有(一)點兒 yǒu (yì)diǎnr (A) some-
　　　　　 what, rather

慢　màn (SV) slow

性子 xìngzi (N) temper

連...也/都... lián ...yě/dōu...
　　　　　　 (CV) even (including)

比較 bǐjiào (V) compare
　　　　 (A) comparatively,
　　　　　　 rather

急　jí (SV) impatient, anxious,
　　　 hasty, urgent

不得了 bùdéliǎo (SV) terrible,
　　　　　 disastrous
　　　　 (SV comp) awfully,
　　　　　 terribly

唱　chàng (V) sing

歌(兒) gē(r) (N) song
　唱歌(兒) chàng-gē(r) (V-O) sing
　　　　　 (a song)

整天 zhěngtiān (TW) all day long

一塊兒 yíkuàir (A) together (=
　　　　 yìqǐ)

形影不離 xíng-yǐng bù lí (set
　　　　 phrase) inseparable (as
　　　　 form and shadow)

-得多 -de duō (SV comp) (by) a lot;
　　　　　　 much — er

好奇 hàoqí (SV) curious, inquisitive

各　gè (AT) each, all, various,
　　　 different
　各種各樣 gè zhǒng gè yàng
　　　　　 all sorts of

有的 yǒude (SP) some (always used
　　　　 as AT)

道理 dàolǐ (N) reason, sense,
　　　　 principle
　有道理 yǒu-dàolǐ (=SV) reason-
　　　　 able, justified

奇怪 qíguài (SV) strange, odd

回答 huídá (V/N) answer, reply

雨　yǔ (N) rain
　下雨 xià-yǔ (V-O) to rain

窗戶 chuānghu (N) window

差　chà (SV) poor, substandard

糊塗 hútu (SV) muddled, silly

大人 dàren (N) adult, grown-up

麻煩 máfan (SV) troublesome,
　　　　 annoying
　　　 (V) put sb. to trouble
　　　 (N) trouble, bother

記　jì (V) memorize, remember,
　　　 record

部首 bùshǒu (N) radical (of a
　　　　 Chinese character)

比方 bǐfang (N) example
　比方說 bǐfang shuō (IE) for example

三點水 sān diǎn shuǐ (N) 'water'
　　　　　　 radical

關係 guānxi (N) relation(ship),
　　　　 relevance
　A 跟 B 有關係　A is connected
　　　　　 with B

林　lín (BF) forest, woods (in com-
　　　 pound words)

木　mù (BF) tree, wood (in compound
　　　 words)

X字旁 X-zìpáng (N) lateral radical X

樹木 shùmù (N) trees

有意思 yǒu-yìsi (SV) interesting

明白 míngbai (SV) clear, plain,
　　　　 obvious
　　　 (V) understand

嘴　zuǐ (N) mouth

茶杯 chábēi (N) teacup

木頭 mùtou (N) wood (the material)

杯子 bēizi (N) cup, glass

笨　bèn (SV) stupid, obtuse, clumsy

意思 yìsi (N) meaning; idea; inten-
　　　　 tion; opinion
　對 X 有意思　have designs on X

才　cái (A) only, merely

白　bái (SV) white; fair, pale (of
　　　 complexion)

沒關係 méi guānxi (IE) it doesn't
　　　　 matter; never mind

住在我們三樓的老張夫婦有兩個男孩子,大的八歲,小的六歲.兄弟倆都是蘋果臉兒,大眼睛,長得像極了.雖然哥哥比弟弟高一點兒,弟弟比哥哥胖一點兒,可是還有不少人以為他們是雙生兄弟.這兩個孩子一樣聰明,一樣可愛,不過他們的性情完全不同.哥哥有點兒像父親,是個慢性子:說話說得慢,走路走得慢,連吃飯也吃得慢.弟弟比較像母親,是個急性子,做甚麼事都急得不得了:看書看得快,寫字寫得快,連跟小朋友一起唱歌兒也比別人唱得快.兩兄弟從小就玩兒得很好,整天在一塊兒,形影不離.哥哥雖然只比弟弟大兩歲,可是知道的事情好像比弟弟多得多.弟弟非常好奇,各種各樣的問題多極了.有的問得很有道理;有的奇怪得誰也沒法子回答.那天外頭雨下得很大,不能出去玩兒.哥哥坐在窗戶旁邊兒看書,弟弟一邊兒寫字,一邊兒跟哥哥說話:

DIALOGUE

A: 哥,你來看看我這幾個字寫得好不好.

B: 你是怎麼寫的?!今天比昨天寫得更差了.

A: 為甚麼我的字總是這麼難看呢?我真不想寫了!

B: 寫字不能太快,你寫得太快了.

A: 可是爸爸比我寫得快得多,為甚麼寫得那麼好?

B: 你真糊塗!爸是大人,小孩兒怎麼能跟大人比?!

A: 哥,中國字真麻煩.我記得快,忘得也快,你有甚麼好法子嗎?

B: 我們老師說學一個字應該先記這個字的部首.比方說'湖'這個字有三點水兒,一定跟水有關係;'林'這個字是'木'字旁兒,一定跟樹木有關係.

A: 這真有意思,現在我才明白為甚麼'吃'跟'喝'都是'口'字旁兒.

B: 當然了,要是沒有嘴,怎麼吃、怎麼喝啊?

A: 可是茶杯的'杯'字兒,為甚麼是'木'字旁兒呢?我從來沒見過木頭做的杯子.

B: 你真笨,怎麼連這個都不懂!你看'杯'這個字,一邊兒是'木',一邊兒是'不',意思就是說杯子不是木頭做的!

SKETCHES

(1)

A: 你的漢語說得真漂亮!

B: 說得不好,我不會說。

A: 你在這兒學了幾年了?

B: 我才學了四個月。

A: 四個月就說得這麼流利,真不容易!你們一個星期學幾課?

B: 我們學得非常快,有的時候學兩課,有的時候學三課。

A: 這是你寫的漢字吧?寫得真好。

B: 難看極了,您別看了。

A: 你們那位老師教得怎麼樣?

B: 教得好極了,每一個字,每一句話,都解釋得很清楚。

A: 我跟你們老師住得很近,常常見面,你知道嗎?

B: 當然知道,要是不知道我就不這麼說了。

(2)

A: 李家兩姐妹,姐姐比妹妹大幾歲?

B: 只大一歲半。

A: 是不是姐姐書念得比妹妹好?

B: 不錯,妹妹雖然比姐姐聰明一點兒,可是姐姐比妹妹用功得多。

A: 姐妹倆誰比較漂亮?

B: 這就很難說了。兩個人長得都很好看,姐姐比妹妹高一點兒,妹妹比姐姐白一點兒。

A: 兩個人誰比誰能幹?

B: 都很能幹。姐姐做家裏的事比妹妹做得快,妹妹出去辦事比姐姐辦得好。

A: 你比較喜歡誰?

B: 我喜歡誰都沒用,因為他們姐妹倆都不喜歡我。

A: 噢!真對不起,我以為……

B: 沒關係,我本來對她們也沒意思!

SPEECH PATTERNS

(1) Predicative complements

Patterns: a.   V <u>de</u> SV (<u>bu</u> SV)   V <u>de</u> A SV

他説得 流(利)不流利 ？ 他説得不太流利.

b.   V O V <u>de</u> (A) SV

他説漢語説得 很流利.

or   O V <u>de</u> (A) SV

他漢語説得 很 流利.

1. 今天他來得早不早?   很早,七點鐘就來了.

2. 他吃飯吃得很慢嗎?   他吃飯吃得不慢,做事做得很慢.

3. 你甚麼地方不舒服嗎?
   沒有不舒服,不過這兩天晚上睡得不太好.

4. 昨天你不在家嗎?
   我帶孩子上公園兒去了,在那兒玩得很高興.

5. 你好像精神不大好.   最近太忙了,休息得不夠.

6. 這個問題他解釋得清不清楚?   他解釋得非常清楚.

7. 你歌兒唱得怎麼樣?   對不起,我甚麼歌兒都不會唱.

8. 他開車開得好不好?   開得不錯,就是開得比較快,沒人敢坐.

9. 第十二課的錄音你們聽了嗎?
   聽了,錄得很不好,一會兒慢一會兒快.

10. 她中國菜做得怎麼樣?   她做得又快又好.

11a. 他買的那些東西都很貴。 b. 他買得貴.

12a. 他説的沒人懂.   b. 他説得很明白.

(2) Intensifying complements

Patterns: a.   SV <u>de</u> hěn

天氣冷得很.

b.   SV <u>jíle</u>

天氣冷極了.

c.   SV <u>de</u> <u>bùdéliǎo</u>

天氣冷得 不得了.

d.   SV <u>de</u> Clause

天氣冷得誰都不想出去.

1. 他運氣好得很,剛到車站,車就來了.
2. 這個人的性情(奇)怪得很,他從來不跟人說話.
3. 昨天我看的那個電影兒有意思極了.
4. 她中國話說得流利極了.
5. 你們星期六在老王家玩兒得怎麼樣?
   我們玩兒得高興極了.
6. 外頭冷得不得了,裏頭熱得不得了,哪兒都不舒服.
7. 她說做這個菜最少得三天,麻煩得不得了.
8. 這個人糊塗得不得了,你跟他說甚麼,他都說"有道理,有道理".
9. 今天整整忙了一天,我現在累得甚麼都不想做了.
10. 那個小女孩兒,大眼睛小嘴兒,漂亮得人見人愛.
11. 兩天沒吃飯,他餓得不能再走了.
12. 昨天雨大得我們沒法子出去.

(3) <u>Comparison</u>

Patterns:　a.　A　(neg)　<u>bǐ</u>　B　SV　(<u>ma</u>?)
　　　　　　他　(不)　比我　慢.
　　　　　b.　A　V　O　V　<u>de</u>　(neg)　<u>bǐ</u>　B　SV
　　　　　　他　寫字寫得　(不)　比　我　慢.
　　　or　A　V　O　(neg)　<u>bǐ</u>　B　V　<u>de</u>　SV
　　　　　　他　寫字　(不)　比我　寫得　慢.
　　　or　A　O　V　<u>de</u>　(neg)　<u>bǐ</u>　B　SV
　　　　　　他　字寫得　(不)　比我　慢.

1. 漢語比英語難吧?　　差不多,都不容易.
2. 他是不是比你又高又胖?　　他比我高,可是不比我胖.
3. 這兩所兒房子,哪所兒好?
   很難說,這所兒比那所兒大,那所兒比這所兒漂亮.
4. 他們夫婦倆,誰的性情好?　　先生的性情比太太好.
5. 這件事誰去辦比較好?　　你去比他去好.
6. 他跑得比你快嗎?　　他跑得比誰都快./他比誰都跑得快.
7. 弟弟比哥哥聰明嗎?　　聰明,弟弟學得比哥哥又快又好.
8. 你怎麼總是比別人累?　　我睡得比他們都少.

9. 你牌打得不錯吧?　　我不怎麼會打,他們打得都比我好.

10. 他信寫得好不好?　　寫得有意思極了,寫得比我們都好.

11. 這個問題她們倆都回答了嗎?

　　都回答了,姐姐回答得比妹妹清楚.

12. 你們為甚麼比別人賣得貴?　　我們的東西比別人好.

(4) Comparison with 'gèng' and 'hái'

Pattern:　　　　　　A　bǐ　B gèng/hái　SV
　　他很高,可是他弟弟 比 他　 更 　高.

1. 你比我聰明,可是他比你更聰明.

2. 你說得不錯,不過他比你更有道理.

3. 說中國話已經夠麻煩了,寫漢字比說中國話更麻煩.

4. 王大夫是不是倫敦最有名的大夫?

　　不是,李大夫比他更有名.

5. 他比你忘得快,可是我比他忘得更快.

6. 她又聰明又用功,中國話說得比中國人還好.

7. 他弟弟騎車騎得比汽車還快.

8. 這個字他學了三百次了還不認識,真是比牛還笨!

(5) Degrees of comparison

Patterns: a.　A　bǐ　B　SV　yìdiǎnr
　　　　　　他 比 我 胖 一點兒.
　　　　 b.　A　bǐ　B　SV　de duō
　　　　　　他 比 我 胖 得多.
　　　　 c.　A　bǐ　B　SV　duōle
　　　　　　他 比 我 胖 多了.
　　　　 d.　A　bǐ　B　SV　NU M
　　　　　　他 比 我 胖 八公斤.

1. 你說住樓上好,還是住樓下好?

　　大概住樓上(比住樓下)好一點兒.

2. 前頭的窗戶大,還是後頭的窗戶大?

　　前頭的(比後頭的)大一點兒.

3. 你們倆的英文誰說得流利?　　她(說得)比我流利得多.

4. 你比他聰明吧?　　不不不,我比他笨得多.

5. 今天是不是比昨天冷點兒?　　今天比昨天冷多了!

6. 他寫得比從前好嗎?　　比從前差多了,不能比.

7. 你比你妹妹大幾歲?　　只大一歲三個月.

8. 你的錶快不快?　　不快,比學校的鐘慢兩分.

9. 這種比那種貴多少?　　貴一塊半.

10. 他的錢比你多多少?　　一個月多十二塊.

11. 她教書教得比你久吧?　　對了,她教得比我久一點兒.

12. 你弟弟比你長得高吧?　　他高多了,比我整整高一個頭.

13. 他還是跑得很慢嗎?　　最近他天天練跑,比以前跑得快多了.

14. 她解釋得清不清楚?　　很清楚,比老師解釋得清楚得多.

(6) 'Lián ... yě/dōu ...' construction

Patterns:　a.　Lián　S　yě/dōu　V　O
　　　　　　　　連　他　　都　知道這件事.
　　　　　　b.　S　lián　O　yě/dōu　V
　　　　　　　　他　連　這件事　都　知道.

1. 今天忙極了,我連午飯都沒時間吃.
2. 他聰明得不得了,連電腦都比他慢.
3. 這個問題太簡單了,連三歲的小孩兒都知道怎麼回答.
4. 他會說幾句中國話,可是連半個漢字都不認識.
5. 我今天連一分錢都沒帶,怎麼能下館子?
6. 你上樓找誰?樓上連一個人都沒有.
7. 你怎麼笨得連北京在哪兒都不知道?!
8. 他糊塗得連自己姓甚麼都忘了.
9. 我們高興得連課也不想上了.
10. 她急得連飯都沒吃就走了.
11. 他們玩兒得連時間都忘了.
12. 他喝得連東南西北都不知道了.

(7) **'Yìdiǎnr' and 'yǒu yìdiǎnr' contrasted**

Patterns: a.　　A　(bǐ B)　SV (yì)diǎnr　　(Comparison)
　　　　　這個 (比那個)大 (一)點兒.
　　　　b.　　A　yǒu (yì)diǎnr SV　　(Adverb)
　　　　　這個有 (一)點兒大.

1a. 今天(比昨天)冷一點兒.

　b. 今天有點兒冷.

2a. 他的性情(比他愛人)急一點兒.

　b. 他人不錯,可是性情有點兒急.

3a. 這件事(比那件事/比別的事)麻煩點兒.

　b. 這件事有點兒麻煩.

4a. 要是他(比現在)高一點兒,就更像他哥哥了.

　b. 他長得有點兒像他哥哥.

5. 孩子們都有點兒好奇,所以常常問大人沒法子回答的問題.

6. 這個人有點兒糊塗,連自己家多少號都不知道.
　 (Contrast:　這個人比較聰明.)

7. 我覺得這課有點兒難.
　 (Contrast:　他覺得這課很容易.)

8. 他說的那個辦法有點兒奇怪.
　 (Contrast:　她說的那個辦法很有道理.)

9. 你說別人都比他用功,他好像有點兒不高興.
　 (Contrast:　她今天好像很高興.)

10. 他今天有點兒不舒服,不能來上課.
　 (Contrast:　她今天精神好得很.)

接	jiē (V) to join; to receive (mail); to meet (welcome) sb.; to answer the phone	搬	bān (V) to move
封	fēng (V) to seal (M) for letters 信封 (N) envelope	鄉	xiāng (鄉)'鄉'[乡] * countryside; rural
郵	yóu ⌈邮⌉ * postal (V) to post, to mail 郵票 postal stamp	和	hé (C) and (CV) with
貼	tiē ⌈贴⌉ (V) to stick (on), to paste	鄰	lín '隣' * ⌈邻⌉ neighbour鄰居; neighbouring; adjacent
龍	lóng ⌈龙⌉ (N) dragon (M:條) a surname	居	jū * to reside; to dwell; to be (in a certain position)
鳳	fèng ⌈凤⌉ (N) phoenix (M:隻)	考	kǎo (V) to give/take an examina- tion
舞	wǔ (N) dance * to dance	藝	yì * ⌈艺⌉ skill; art 文藝 literature and art
潑	pō ⌈泼⌉ (V) to sprinkle; to splash; to spill (SV) shrewish	術	shù '術' * ⌈术⌉ skill; technique; method; tactics 美術 fine arts
力	lì * strength; power; force; ability	相	xiāng * each other; mutually
寄	jì (V) to send (by post) * to entrust	拿	ná (V) to take in the hand; to take hold of (CV) with
原	yuán * primary; original; former; unprocessed	入	rù (V) to enter; to join 入口 entrance
畫	huà ⌈画⌉ (V) to draw; to paint 畫兒 (N) picture, painting	另	lìng (A) other; another; separ- ately

世	shì ‘丗’ * world 世界 (M) a generation/lifetime	舊	jiù　　　　[旧] (SV) old (opp. of 新) (AT) second-hand; used; 　former
界	jiè　　　　* boundary; realm; scope; circles (as 文藝界)	古	gǔ (SV) ancient, age-old
如	rú　　　　* like, as; as if; such as 不如 not equal to; not as good as; inferior to	拉	lā (V) to pull; to draw; to play (a bowed instrument)
倒	dào (A) indeed; actually; as it happens (contrary to expec- tation)	簾	lián (簾) *　[帘] hanging screen; curtain 簾子 窗簾 window curtains
許	xǔ　　　　[许] (V) to permit, to allow 也許 perhaps; maybe a surname	陽	yáng　　　　[阳] (N) the masculine or posi- tive principle in nature 太陽 the sun
預	yù　　　　*　[预] in advance, beforehand	吹	chuī (V) to blow; to boast 吹牛; to play (wind instruments); to fall through (of plans)
備	bèi　　　　*　[备] to prepare	燈	dēng　　　　[灯] (N) lamp; light
幅	fú (M) for pictures, paintings; 　width of cloth	實	shí　　　　*　[实] solid; true; real; fact 實在 really, truly
特	tè　　　　* special(ly)	試	shì　　　　[试] (V) to try; to test 考試 examination; test 口試 oral examination
街	jiē (N) street　　　(M:條) 街道 streets (collective) 大街 main street	步	bù * on foot (M) a step; a move in a 　board game

接	扌 扩 拉 接	[手扌]
封	土 圭 封	[寸]
郵	丿 二 三 垂 垂 垂 垂 郵	[邑阝]
(邮)	日 由 邮	
貼	貝 貼 貼 (贴)	[貝]
龍	立 音 音 竜 竜 龍 龍	[龍]
(龙)	一 ナ 尤 龙 龙	
鳳	丿 几 凡 凤 凤 鳳 鳳	[鳥]
(凤)	丿 几 凤	
舞	一 二 無 無 舞 舞 舞 舞	[舛]
潑	氵 氵 氵 氵 潑 潑 潑	[水氵]
(泼)	氵 氵 氵 泼 泼 泼	
力	フ 力	[力]
寄	宀 宲 寄 寄	[宀]
原	厂 厂 盾 原	[厂]
畫	一 聿 聿 書 畫 畫	[田]
(画)	一 面 画 画	
搬	扌 扣 扣 抈 拥 搬	[手扌]
鄉	乡 乡 乡 乡 乡 乡 绲 鄉	[邑阝]
(乡)	乡 乡 乡	
和	禾 和	[口]
鄰	米 粦 粦 舜 鄰	[邑阝]
(邻)	人 令 邻	
居	尸 尸 屏 居	[尸]
考	土 耂 耂 考	[老]
藝	艹 艺 芸 蓺 蓺 蓺 藝	[艸艹]
(艺)	艹 艺	

術	彳 彳 彳 彳 術 術 (术)	[行]
相	木 相	[目]
拿	人 合 拿	[手]
入	丿 入	[入]
另	口 号 另	[口]
世	一 廿 廿 世	[一]
界	田 界 界	[田]
如	女 如	[女]
倒	亻 倅 倅 倒	[人亻]
許	言 計 許 許 (许)	[言]
預	マ 予 予 預 (预)	[頁]
備	亻 亻 亻 伊 俏 備 備 (备)	[人亻]
幅	口 巾 帄 幅	[巾]
特	牛 牛 牛 特	[牛牜]
街	彳 彳 往 街	[行]
舊	艹 萑 萑 舊 舊 (旧)	[臼]
古	一 十 古	[口]
拉	扌 拉	[手扌]
簾	艹 芦 芦 箐 箐 簾 簾	[竹艹]
(帘)	宀 穴 帘	
陽	阝 阳 阴 陽 陽 (阳)	[阜阝]
吹	口 吣 吹	[口]
燈	火 灯 灯 烣 燈 燈 (灯)	[火]
實	宀 宀 宲 宲 實 實	[宀]
(实)	宀 宀 宝 实 实	
試	言 計 計 試 試 (试)	[言]
步	丨 卜 止 止 止 步 步	[止]

VOCABULARY

前天 qiántiān (TW) day before yesterday

接(到) jiē(dào) (V) receive

封 fēng (M) measure for letters (V) seal

郵票 yóupiào (N) postage stamp

貼 tiē (V) stick (on)

信封 xìnfēng (N) envelope

毛筆 máobǐ (N) brush (for writing)

龍飛鳳舞 lóng-fēi fèng-wǔ (set phrase) 'dragon flies, phoenix dances': flamboyant

活潑 huópo (SV) lively, vivacious

有力 yǒu-lì (SV) forceful

當時 dāngshí (TW) then, at that time

寄 jì (V) send, post

當中 dāngzhōng (PW) among, in the middle

等到 děngdào (TW) by the time, when ('wait till')

打開 dǎkāi (V) open

發現 fāxiàn (V) discover

原來 yuánlái (MA) originally; as a matter of fact, actually

畫家 huàjiā (N) painter

搬(到) bān(dào) (V) move (to)

鄉下 xiāngxia (PW) country (as opposed to town)

和 hé (C/CV) and, with (similar to gēn 跟)

鄰居 línjū (N) neighbour

畫兒 huàr (N) painting, picture

念完 niànwán (V) finish studying

-完 -wán (V comp) finish —ing

畫畫兒 huà-huàr (V-O) to paint, to draw

考 kǎo (V) give/take an examination, test

考上 kǎoshàng — (V) pass exam for —

藝術 yìshù (N) art (SV) artistic

學院 xuéyuàn (N) college

相當 xiāngdāng (A) quite, considerably, pretty

專心 zhuānxīn (SV) single-minded, engrossed

只要 zhǐyào (MA) it only needs; if only; as long as ....

一 ... 就... yī ... jiù ... once/as soon as ... then...

拿 ná (V) take in the hand, hold

拿起來 náqilai (V) pick up

進入 jìnrù (V) enter into

另外 lìngwài (A) besides, separately (AT) another

世界 shìjiè (N) world

面前 miànqián (PW) in front of, in face of

如果 rúguǒ (MA) if (= yàoshi 要是)

簡直 jiǎnzhí (A) simply

睡不着 shuìbuzháo (V) unable to get to sleep

-着 -zháo (V comp) get to (indicates attainment of objective)

怪人 guàiren (N) strange person, eccentric

倒(是) dào(shi) (A) indeed, actually, as it happens (marks something contrary to the general drift or line of thought)

談得來 tándelái (V) able to talk to/get on with

本 běn (SP) this, the present

也許 yěxǔ (MA) perhaps

預備 yùbèi (V) prepare, make ready

叫門 jiào mén (VO) call at the door (to be let in)

說不定 shuōbudìng (V) can't say for sure
(MA) maybe

果然 guǒrán (MA) sure enough, just as predicted

大半天 dà bàntiān (TW) greater half of a day; 'ages'

幅 fú (M) for paintings; width (of cloth)

門外漢 ménwàihàn (N) layman

特別 tèbié (SV/A) special(ly), particular(ly)

叫好 jiào-hǎo (V-O) 'shout well-done'; applaud

街 jiē (N) street

舊 jiù (SV) old; second-hand; former

古 gǔ (SV) old, ancient

關 guān (V) close, shut up/in, turn off

關上 guānshang (V) close to

拉 lā (V) pull

拉上 lāshang (V) pull to

窗簾(兒) chuānglián(r) (N) window curtains

見不得 jiànbudé (V) may not be seen by/ exposed to

太陽 tàiyáng (N) sun

吹 chuī (V) blow

吹不得 chuībudé (V) may not be blown (by)

風 fēng (N) wind

開 kāi (V) open; turn on

燈 dēng (N) lamp, light

客氣 kèqi (SV) polite; formal; modest in manner

不(要)客氣 (IE) don't mention it! please don't bother

實在 shízài (A) in reality, honestly, really

筆 bǐ (M) stroke (with a pen or brush)

老兄 lǎo xiōng (N) (form of address between male friends) 'old chap'

考試 kǎoshì (N/V) (have an) examination

進步 jìnbù (V/N/SV) progress; progressive

一般 yìbān (SV/A) general, common, ordinary; generally, equally (used before SV)

不好意思 bù-hǎoyìsi (IE) embarrassed, ill at ease

PRESENTATION

前天中午我忽然接到一封不知從哪兒來的信,連郵票也沒貼.信封上的字是用毛筆寫的,龍飛鳳舞,活潑有力.當時我想不出這封信是誰寄給我的,因為我的朋友當中沒有一個能寫得了這麼漂亮的毛筆字.等到打開信才發現原來是老高寫來的.沒想到兩年不見,我這位畫家朋友的字已經練得這麼好了.老高搬到鄉下去以前和我是鄰居.他五歲開始學畫兒,中學沒念完就考上了藝術學院,現在已經相當有名了.他畫畫兒的時候非常專心,只要一拿起筆來就好像進入了另外一個世界.誰走過他面前,他也看不見,誰跟他說話,他也聽不見.如果一張畫兒沒畫完,他簡直飯也吃不下,覺也睡不着.朋友們都說他是個怪人.我雖然不懂藝術,可是跟他倒很談得來.他信上說本月十八號要進城,如果有時間,也許來看我.今天就是十八號,我已經預備好了飯菜,他怎麼還不來呢?欸,你聽,外頭有人叫門,說不定就是老高......

DIALOGUE

A: 來了,來了,聽見了! 誰啊?

B: 我啊,猜得出我是誰嗎?

A: 老高,果然是你!快進來,快進來,已經等你大半天了.吃過飯沒有?

B: 怎麼?一進門就要請我吃飯? 別急,別急,請你先看看我帶來的這幅畫兒.

A: 你知道我對畫兒完全是門外漢,甚麼也看不懂.

B: 這幅畫兒很特別,我敢說你看完了一定叫好.今天運氣真不錯,沒想到在東大街那家舊書店買到了這麼一幅古畫兒.

A: 噢!是剛買的,那麼就請你快點兒拿出來吧.

B: 不行,得先麻煩你關上窗户,拉上窗簾兒.

A: 為甚麼?這幅畫兒有甚麼見不得人的地方嗎?

B: 你看你想到哪兒去了!這幅古畫兒已經有三百年了,不是見不得人,是見不得太陽,吹不得風,請你快開開燈吧!

A: 這畫的是竹子嗎?我怎麼看不清楚?老高啊,說句不客氣的話,我實在不知道這幅畫兒好在哪裏.

B: 你看,你看這一筆,就這一筆最少也得二十年的功夫.

A: 二十年的功夫?!對不起,我看不出來.

B: 老兄啊,要想看得出來,恐怕也得二十年!

SKETCHES

(1) A: 哥,你在樓上嗎?看見今天的報沒有?

B: 在我這兒,我還沒看完呢.

A: 你還要多久才能看完?先拿下來給我看看行不行?

B: 你想看報?!你的練習做完了嗎?

A: 吃飯以前就做完了.

B: 你不是說明天考試嗎?都預備好了嗎?

A: 早就預備好了.

B: 昨天那個數學問題還沒搞清楚吧.

A: 搞清楚了.

B: 欸,剛才媽叫你上街去買魚,買到了嗎?

A: 已經買回來了.

B: 那...那麼你想幹麼?

A: 我不想幹麼,只想看看今天的報.

(2) A: 你中文學得怎麼樣了?進步很快吧?

B: 不行,我學得比一般人都慢,簡單的話雖然能聽懂不少了,可是一開口,就常常說錯,真不好意思!

A: 你別不好意思了,我們中國人說英文的時候錯得更多.你這麼用功一定可以學得好.

B: 不用功不行啊!你看我們一天就有這麼多練習,我不睡覺也做不完.

A: 別着急,你已經學得不錯了.我們去食堂吃飯吧.

B: 這些練習沒做完,我甚麼也吃不下.

A: 不吃飯怎麼能有精神學習呢?

B: 那就麻煩你替我買一塊三明治好不好?

A: 一塊三明治吃得飽嗎? 兩塊吧.

B: 不,一塊就夠了.你不知道,我一吃飽了就想睡覺,更沒法子學了.

<u>SPEECH PATTERNS</u>

(1) <u>Resultative complements</u>

(a) Some common resultative complements

Complements	Stem verbs
-見 (sensory perception)	看,聽,碰...
-到 (arrival, attainment)	看,找,走,買,寄,送,想,學...
-着 (attainment)	找,見,買,睡...
-完 (completion)	做,說,吃,寫...
-好 (satisfaction, completion)	做,寫,辦,預備...
-會 (learning mastery)	學,搞...
-懂 (understanding)	看,聽,搞...
-開 (detachment, separation)	開,打,拉...
-定 (definiteness)	說...
-住 (fixity, secureness)	拿,記,貼...
-對 (correctness)	做,說,寫,搞...
-錯 (error)	做,說,寫,搞...

-清楚 (clarity) 　　　　　說,寫,看...

-飽 (repleteness) 　　　　吃,喝...

(b) Use of resultative complements

　　Pattern: 你接到我的信了嗎?
　　　or　　你接到我的信沒有?　　接到了./沒接到.

1. 你看,山上有兩個人.　　我早就看到了,好像是老張和小李.
2. 你聽外頭有人叫你.　　是嗎?我怎麼沒聽見?你聽錯了吧!
3. 孩子們都上樓睡覺了嗎?　　都上去了,已經睡着了.
4. 老王昨天做的魚怎麼樣?　　聽說好吃極了,我去晚了,沒吃着.
5. 這本小說你快看完了吧?　　我才看了一半,也許明天可以看完.
6. 那張畫兒你還沒畫好吧?　　畫好了,不過畫得非常不好.
7. 你們明天到鄉下去,預備好了嗎?
　　差不多都預備好了,希望明天別下雨.
8. 你學過太極拳嗎?　　學過,可是沒學會.
9. 他寫的字龍飛鳳舞,很不容易看懂.
　　容易看懂就不夠藝術了.
10. 開門,開門,我回來了!　　門已經開開了,快進來吧!
11. 他這個字是不是寫錯了?
　　你開開燈我看看,是沒寫對,這兒少了一筆.
12. 那個地方很好找,你只要記住在圖書館的東邊兒就行了.
13. 剛才收音機上是不是說明天有大風?　　我沒聽清楚.
14. 我們已經說定了,誰先做完練習誰去買東西.
15. 我發現除了他以外,還有另外一個人也看到了這件事.

(2) Directional complements

(a) Some common directional complements

Complements	Stem verbs
-上 (up; on; attainment)	關,拉,戴,考...

-下　(down; having room for)　　　坐,吃 …

-來　(in this direction)　　　上,下,進,出,回,拿,送,帶,寄,搬 …

-去　(in that direction)　　　(ditto)

-進　(in, into)　　　搬,拿,帶,跑,走 …

-出　(out)　　　(ditto)

-到　(arrive)　　　走,跑,學,寄,搬,拿 …

-過　(pass)　　　走,吃,看 …

-走　(away)　　　拿,搬,帶,送 …

-上來　(come up)　　　拿,搬,送,跑,走 …

-下來　(come down)　　　(ditto)

-上去　(go up)　　　(ditto)

-下去　(go down)　　　(ditto)

-進來　(come in)　　　(ditto)

-出來　(come out)　　　(ditto)

-進去　(go in)　　　(ditto)

-出去　(go out)　　　(ditto)

-起來　(rise, get up)　　　想,拿 …

(b) Use of directional complements

Patterns: a.　　　V　DC　O
　　　他關上窗戶,拉上窗簾,就去睡覺了.
　　　b.　　V　DC　O　(lai / qu)
　　　他拿出一幅畫兒來 請大家看.

1. 他戴上錶,關上門,就出去了.
2. 坐下,坐下,有話坐下再說.
3. 如果你沒時間送來,寄來也可以.
4. 你弟弟去年考大學沒有？ 考了,可是沒考上.
5. 寄到中國去的信得貼多少錢的郵票？
6. 我以為那家書店還在老地方,原來他們已經搬到另外一條街上去了
7. 他用功得不得了,每天晚上都要念到一、兩點.
8. 你常碰見他嗎？ 我們是鄰居,常碰見,我每天都得走過他家門口兩次

9. 吃過飯了嗎?　　吃過了,連咖啡都喝過了.
10. 你心裏有甚麽話,請你都説出來吧!
11. 學生們正要跑出去玩兒的時候,老師從外邊兒走進來了.
12. 原來住在那兒的人已經搬走了,我們打算下月三號搬進去.
13. 你看見他那幅古畫兒了嗎?
　　他本來已經拿出來了,看見你來,又拿回去了.
14. 他説的話你們都寫下來了嗎?　　每個字都寫下來了.
15. 她這封信的意思,你看出來了沒有?
　　我沒看出來有甚麽特別的意思.
16. 我今天帶的錢不夠,得回家去再拿點兒來.
17. 我剛走進去,他就拿起一份報來叫我看.
18. 你不是已經睡覺了嗎? 怎麽又跑下樓來了?
　　我忽然想起一件事來...

(3) <u>Potential complements</u>

(a) Some common potential complements

Affirmative	Negative	
見得	見不得	can be seen; be obvious/cannot be presented to
吃得	吃不得	may/may not be eaten
聽得見	聽不見	can/cannot hear
找得到	找不到	can/cannot find
睡得着	睡不着	can/cannot get to sleep
做得完	做不完	can/cannot finish doing
學得好	學不好	can/cannot master
看得懂	看不懂	can/cannot make out, understand, read
記得住	記不住	can/cannot remember
辦得了	辦不了	can/cannot carry out
吃得飽	吃不飽	can/cannot eat one's fill
——	説不定	cannot say for sure
談得來	談不來	can/cannot get along with

考得上	考不上	can/cannot pass the exam for
坐得下	坐不下	can/cannot sit down or seat
上得去	上不去	can/cannot go up
下得去	下不去	can/cannot go down
走得上去	走不上去	can/cannot walk up
吃得下去	吃不下去	can/cannot carry on eating or get food down
看得出來	看不出來	can/cannot detect
開得進去	開不進去	can/cannot drive in
對得起	對不起	not let/let (someone) down

(b) Use of potential complements

Patterns： a. 你看得懂中文嗎？

b. 你看得懂看不懂中文？

看得懂／看不懂．

1. 你看房子上有兩個人． 在哪兒啊？我怎麼看不見？
2. 練習做完了嗎？ 還沒呢，這麼多，恐怕今天做不完．
3. 中國人說話你能聽得懂嗎？
   如果說的是普通話，我也許能聽得懂．
4. 這麼熱，快開開窗戶吧！ 我剛才開了半天，開不開．
5. 我想買一幅中國畫兒，不知道在這兒買得着買不着．
6. 世界上的事情真奇怪，想吃飽的人吃不飽;可以吃飽的人不吃飽
7. 這件事他一個人去辦得了辦不了？ 他那麼能幹，一定辦得了
8. 這麼難寫的字，你記得住記不住？ 不必問，當然記不住．
9. 我和老王從小就很談得來，現在還是好朋友．
10. 今天星期天不上班，甚麼人也找不到．
11. 明天我們學得到第十五課嗎？ 說不定，也許學得到．
12. 如果明年你能考上大學.... 別'如果'了，我一定考不上．
13. 她這兩天心裏有事，飯也吃不下，覺也睡不着．
14. 這個地方坐得下一百個人嗎？
    坐不下，最多只能坐下三十個人．
15. 他們住在八樓，你走得上去嗎？ 我這麼胖，恐怕走不上去．

16. 三明治太難吃了,我簡直吃不下去.
17. 你看得出來這是誰寫的字嗎?　　噢!我沒看出這是字來.
18. 大門太小,汽車開不進去,怎麼辦?　　我也想不出甚麼辦法來.
19. 你的畫兒能不能拿出來給我們看看?
　　不行,不行,我的畫兒實在見不得人.
20. 您別客氣再吃一點兒吧!
　　謝謝您,我不會客氣,我真的吃飽了,實在吃不下了.

(4) Complement 'guò' and suffix '-guo' contrasted

1a. 你吃過飯了嗎?
 b. 你吃過中國飯嗎?

2a. 今天送信的來過了嗎?　　來過了,沒有你的信.
 b. 他來過英國嗎?　　來過,一九七八年來過一次.

3a. 你已經走過了西門大街,你看後頭那條就是.
 b. 你以前走過西門大街嗎?　　沒有,這是第一次.

4a. 桌子上的菜每樣你都吃過了嗎?　　除了魚以外,我都吃過了.
 b. 桌子上的菜每樣你都吃過嗎?　　有的吃過,有的沒吃過.

5a. 這份中文報我已經看過了,你拿去看吧.
 b. 你看過中文報嗎?　　看過一次,看不懂.

(5) Predicative complements and potential complements contrasted

1a. 他做得好不好?　　大家都說他做得好.
 b. 他做得好做不好?　　他很專心,一定做得好.

2a. 她說得清(楚)不清楚?　　她說得(相當)清楚.
 b. 她說得清楚說不清楚?　　這麼簡單的問題,她說得清楚.

3a. 你比你哥哥跑得快嗎?　　我比他跑得快.
 b. 你跑得快跑不快?　　如果前頭有好吃的東西,我當然跑得快.

139

4a. 這個字他寫得不對.

b. 這個字他寫了十次了,可是還是寫不對.

5a. 他喝得不多,只喝了一杯.

b. 他喝不多,一杯就夠了.

(6) 'Gei' used as a verb complement

Pattern:　　　Vgei　Ind O　Dir O

他寄給　我　一本書.

1. 快吃吧,這是媽特別做給你吃的.
2. 這是他的毛衣,昨天忘在這兒了,麻煩您帶給他好嗎?
3. 你那封信是寫給誰的?
4. 那件事你能不能說給我們聽聽?　　恐怕我說三天也說不完.
5. 我不知道你要買舊車,我已經賣給別人了.
6. 他的那幅中國畫兒已經送給大學圖書館了.
7. 報上的字太小,我看不清楚,請你念給我聽聽.
8. 她想看看我剛買的那本舊書,請你拿給她.
9. 他借給我的那本小說沒甚麼意思,寫得很一般.
10. 聽說你認識那位張小姐,能不能介紹給我弟弟?

(7) Coverb 'gěi' and complement 'gei' contrasted

1a. 那本書我上星期就寄給他了,為甚麼他還沒接到?

b. 那本書我上星期就給他寄去了,為甚麼他還沒接到? (= a)

c. 那本書我上星期就給他寄了,為甚麼那個人還沒接到? (=替他

2a. 那輛車你賣給他了嗎?

b. 那輛車你給他賣了嗎? (= 替他)

3a. 這是他寫給我的另外一封信.

b. 這是他給我寫的另外一封信. (1. = a; 2. =他替我寫的.)

4a. 這份兒是他的,請你拿給他.

 b. 他沒來,請你給他拿一份兒 (＝替他)

5a. 這本書借給我看看,行不行?

 b. 請你給我借本書看看,行不行? (＝替我)

(8) 'YI ... jiù ...'

1. 兩點鐘一到,老師就進來了.

2. 老師一進來,我們就都站起來了.

3. 我們一站起來,老師就說:"請坐,請坐!"

4. 老師一說'請坐',我們就都坐下了.

5. 我們一坐下,老師就開始說中國話了.

6. 老師一開始說中國話,我們就糊塗了.

7. 我們一糊塗,老師就不高興了.

8. 老師一不高興,就不想教了.

9. 老師一不想教,我們就學不好了.

10. 他一看見中國字就想睡覺.

11. 我一看見中國人就說不出話來了.

12. 她一吃中國菜就覺得不舒服.

13. 他一有錢就想上酒館兒.

14. 他一喝酒就要說外國話.

15. 他愛人一聽見他說外國話就想打他.

研	yán　　　　[研] (V) to grind fine * to study, to research	切	qiē (V) to cut, to carve, to 　　slice
究	jiū　　　　　* to investigate; after all 研究 (V/N) study, research	紅	hóng　　　　[红] (SV) red; revolutionary (N) bonus, dividend
越	yuè　　　　　* to pass over; to exceed 越 ... 越 ...　　the more ... the more ...	燒	shāo　　　　[烧] (V) to burn; to roast; to 　　stew in soy sauce
受	shòu (V) to receive; to accept; 　　to suffer, to endure	肉	ròu (肉) (N) meat; flesh; pulp (of 　　fruit)
迎	yíng　　　*　　[迎] to meet, greet, welcome	烤	kǎo (V) to roast; to bake; to 　　heat by the fire
但	dàn (C) but, yet (A) merely, only	鴨	yā　　　　*　　[鸭] duck 鴨子　　　(M: 隻) 烤鴨 roast duck
黃	huáng　　　　[黄] (SV) yellow a surname	炒	chǎo (V) to sauté, to stir-fry
餐	cān '湌' * to eat; food; meal (M) for meals	豆	dòu　　　　* beans, peas 豆子
論	lùn　　　　[论] * to discuss; theory (CV) by (in units of) 不論 no matter, regardless	腐	fǔ　　　　　* rotten, decay 豆腐 bean curd
地	de (K) adverbial marker	嫩	nèn (SV) tender; delicate (of 　　skin)
把	bǎ (V) to hold; to guard (CV) governing object dis- posed of before verb	香	xiāng (SV) fragrant, aromatic; 　　　smell good (of food) (N) incense, incense sticks
當	dàng　　　　[当] (V) to regard as, to treat 　　as; to think (mistakenly) 　　that	花	huā　　　　[花] (N) flower (SV) flowery, fancy, coloured (V) to spend (money, time)

成	chéng (V) to accomplish; to become; to change into (SV) all right, be OK	醬	jiàng '醬' [醬] (N) thick sauce; jam
譜	pǔ [谱] (N) list, chart; manual; score (of music)	油	yóu (N) oil, fat, grease, petrol (SV) oily; glib 醬油 soy sauce
萬	wàn [万] (NU) ten thousand 一萬五(千) 15,000 a surname	素	sù (SV) simple, plain * vegetarian food 素菜 吃素 to be a vegetarian
廚	chú * [厨] kitchen 廚房	奶	nǎi (N) milk; breast 牛奶 cow's milk
陣	zhèn [阵] (M) short period; spell of (N) formation of troops	盤	pán [盘] (N) tray; plate, dish (V) to coil up (M) game of chess, go, etc.
拼	pīn '拚' [拼] (V) to piece together; to spell (words) 拼音 Pinyin	米	mǐ (N) rice (hulled uncooked) * grain (M) metre
手	shǒu (N) hand (M:隻,雙) 好手 good hand, expert (M:把) 第一把手 number one man	筷	kuài chopsticks 筷子 (M:枝,雙)
鍋	guǒ [锅] (N) pot, pan, wok	刀	dāo (N) knife, one-edged sword (M:把) (M) slash (with a knife)
糖	táng (N) sugar; sweets	叉	chā * fork 叉子 (M:把); cross (mark) (V) to fork
醋	cù (N) vinegar; jealousy 吃醋 (VO) feel jealous	敬	jìng (V) to respect; to offer (wine, tea, etc. to a guest)
辣	là (SV) hot (of spices), peppery; ruthless	乾	gān [干] (SV) dry 乾杯 drink a toast; bottoms up, cheers!
鹹	xián [咸] (SV) salty * salted	務	wù [务] * affair; business (LC) be engaged in; must, be sure to
淡	dàn (SV) weak, insipid; light (in colour)	甜	tián (SV) sweet

酸	suān (SV) sour; sore, ache (N) acid	麵	miàn '麵' [面] (N) flour; noodles 麵條兒 炒麵 chow mein
照	zhào (V) to shine on; look at one- self (as in a mirror) (CV) according to, following	鹽	yán '塩' [盐] (N) salt

STROKE-ORDER

研	石 矴 矴 矴 研 (研) 矴 研 [石]	花	艹 花 花 花 (花) [艹]
究	宀 穴 宀 究 [穴]	成	一 厂 瓦 成 成 成 [戈]
越	走 赺 越 越 越 [走]	譜	言 訐 訪 譄 譜 譜 (谱) [言]
受	⺈ ⺈ 受 [又]	萬	艹 莒 萬 萬 萬 (万) [艹]
迎	ノ 𠄌 卬 迎 (迎) [辶]	廚	广 庁 庿 廚 廚 (厨) [广]
但	亻 但 但 [人亻]	陣	阝 阸 陣 (阵) [阜]
黃	一 艹 芒 菁 黃 黃 (黄) [黃]	拼	扌 扩 拌 拌 拼 (拼) 拌 拼 [手扌]
餐	⺊ ⺊ 歺 奴 餐 [食]	手	ノ 二 手 [手]
論	言 訥 訡 諭 論 (论) 论 论 [言]	鍋	金 釘 鍋 鍋 (锅) 钔 铝 锅 [金]
把	扌 扣 扣 扣 把 [手扌]	糖	丷 半 米 粘 粘 粘 糖 糖 [米]
當	丷 ⺍ 当 当 當 (当) [田]	醋	丆 兩 酉 酌 酯 醋 [酉]
切	一 七 切 切 [刀]	辣	丷 ⺁ 立 享 荊 辣 辣 [辛]
紅	糸 紅 (红) [糸]	鹹	⺊ 片 卤 卤 兩 卤 卤 鹹 [鹵]
燒	灶 灶 炲 焼 燒 (烧) 灶 烧 [火]	(咸)	一 厂 石 咸 咸 咸
肉	门 内 肉 [肉]	淡	氵 氵 沙 沙 沙 淡 [水氵]
烤	火 灶 炉 炉 烤 [火]	醬	⺀ ⼿ 犲 狆 將 醬 [酉]
鴨	口 曰 甲 甲 卲 卲 鴨 [鳥]	(醬)	⺀ ⼿ 狆 狆 醬
(鴨)	甲 卲 卲 鴨 鴨	油	氵 汩 汩 油 油 [水氵]
炒	火 灯 炒 炒 [火]	素	二 キ 主 寿 素 [系]
豆	一 石 豆 [豆]	奶	女 奶 奶 [女]
腐	广 庁 府 府 腐 腐 [肉]	盤	舟 舟 舟 般 盤 (盘) [皿]
嫩	女 妁 姉 婞 嫩 [女]	米	丷 丷 半 米 [米]
香	二 千 禾 香 [香]	筷	竹 筑 筤 筷 筷 [竹]

144

刀　フ刀　　　　　　　　[刀]　　甜　一干千舌舌甜甜甜　　[甘]

叉　フ又叉　　　　　　[又]　　酸　酉酉酉酸　　　　　　[酉]

敬　⺌芍芍敬(敬)　　 [攵]　　照　日町昭照　　　　　　[火]

乾　十古車軖乾(干)二干[乙]　麵　十来来麥麥麪麵麵(面)[麥]

務　マ孑予矛敄務(务)　[力]　鹽　一干臣臣臨臨鹽(盐)　[鹵]

VOCABULARY

聞名　wénmíng (SV) renowned (N.B.
　　　　　of restricted use)

　世界聞名　shìjiè wénmíng
　　　　　　 world-famous

研究　yánjiū (V/N) research, study,
　　　　　investigate

越...越...　yuè ... yuè ... (C)
　　　　　the more ... the more...

　越來越...yuè lai yuè ... (A)
　　　　　more and more ...

受歡迎　shòu-huānyíng (SV) be
　　　　popular (receive welcome)

但是　dànshi (C) but, yet

黃　huáng (SV) yellow (a surname)

化學　huàxué (N) chemistry

專家　zhuānjiā (N) expert

思想　sīxiǎng (N) thought, thinking

看法　kànfǎ (N) outlook, view

西化　xīhuà (V/SV) Westernize(d)

　-化　-huà (suffix) -ize, -ify

西餐　xīcān (N) Western food

　餐　cān (BF) food, meal, cuisine
　　　　(M) for meals

吃不來　chībulái (V) unable to
　　　　　take to (foods)

　-來　-lái (V comp) (potential com-
　　　　plement) able to, manage
　　　　to

不論　búlùn (MA) no matter how,
　　　　　regardless

多(麼)　duō(me), duó(me) (A) how, to
　　　　　what extent

好好兒(地)　hǎohāor(de) (A) properly,
　　　　　　thoroughly

　-地　-de (K) adverbial marker

要不然　yàoburán (C) otherwise

把　bǎ (CV) governing object disposed
　　　　of before verb
　　　　(M) for chairs, knives, etc.

當(做)　dàng(zuò) (V) treat as, regard
　　　　　as

白切雞　báiqiējī (N) white/plain cut
　　　　　chicken

紅燒肉　hóngshāoròu (N) red-cooked
　　　　　(pork) meat

烤鴨　kǎoyā (N) roast duck

點心　diǎnxin (N) various pastries
　　　　　and snacks

牛肉　niúròu (N) beef

炒　chǎo (V) stir-fry

豆腐　dòufu (N) bean curd

嫩　nèn (SV) tender, soft

燒　shāo (V) burn; cook, stew, bake

香　xiāng (SV) fragrant
　　　　(N) incense

難得　nán-dé (SV) hard to get, rare

來歷　láilì (N) history, antecedents,
　　　　　origin

為了　wèile (CV) for (the sake of),
　　　　　in order to

花　huā (V) spend (time, money)

工夫　gōngfu (N) time and effort;
　　　　　leisure time

心得　xīndé (N) knowledge gained

有條有理地　yǒu-tiáo-yǒu-lǐde (A) methodically, systematically

寫成　xiěchéng (V) compile (fashion through writing)

　-成　-chéng (V comp) so as to be, become

食譜　shípǔ (N) cookery book

萬　wàn (NU) ten thousand

打進　dǎjìn (V) breach, invade

廚房　chúfáng (N) kitchen

意外(地)　yìwài(de) (A) in an unforeseen manner

陣　zhèn (M) wave, spate, burst, spell

出風頭　chū fēngtou (VO) create a stir, enjoy the limelight

大衣　dàyī (N) overcoat

拼起來　pīnqilai (V) put together

菜單　càidān (N) menu

點(菜)　diǎn (cài) (VO) choose, order (dishes on menu)

拿手　náshǒu (SV) expert in, good at

　拿手菜　náshǒu cài (N) speciality (dish)

家鄉雞　jiāxiāngjī (N) 'home town chicken'

回鍋肉　huíguōròu (N) 'return to the pot meat' — twice-cooked pork

黃魚　huángyú (N) yellow croaker (fish)

來　lái (V) bring (esp. food)

糖醋　tángcù (AT) sweet-and-sour (lit: sugar-vinegar)

辣　là (SV) hot (spices)

鹹　xián (SV) salty, savoury

淡　dàn (SV) bland, mild

放　fàng (V) put; put in; let go

醬油　jiàngyóu (N) soy sauce

記得　jìde (V) remember, recall

素菜　sùcài (N) vegetable dish

奶油菜花　nǎiyóu càihuā (N) creamed cauliflower

　奶油　nǎiyóu (N) cream

拼盤(兒)　pīnpán(r) (N) cold platter

白菜牛肉湯　báicài niúròu tāng (N) cabbage and beef soup

米飯　mǐfàn (N) cooked rice

筷子　kuàizi (N) chopsticks

刀叉　dāo-chā (N) knife and fork

敬　jìng (V) salute, toast

乾杯　gān-bēi (IE) drain glass, Cheers!

服務　fúwù (V/N) serve; service

　服務員　fúwùyuán (N) attendant

甜　tián (SV) sweet

酸　suān (SV) sour

新手　xīnshǒu (N) new hand, novice

照　zhào (CV) according to, in conformity with

不當一回事　bú dàng yì huí shì (IE) not regard as a matter (of any importance)

鍋貼兒　guōtiēr (N) fried dumpling

麵　miàn (N) noodles

公事　gōngshì (N) official business; paperwork

鹽　yán (N) salt

牛奶　niúnǎi (N) (cow) milk

糖　táng (N) sugar; sweets

哪裏　nǎlǐ (IE) Not at all (often reduplicated) = nǎr de huà 哪兒的話

PRESENTATION

中國菜是世界聞名的,因為中國人研究吃的藝術已經有很長的歷史了.最近一、二十年中國菜在英國越來越受歡迎,中國飯館兒也越來越多.雖然這些館子的菜都不錯,但是很少有我朋友黃英白做得那麼好的.老黃是位化學專家,來英國快四十年了,雖然思想和看法都已經相當西化,可是西餐還是吃不來的.每天不論多忙,他也要好好兒地做兩個菜,舒舒服服地吃頓中國飯,要不然晚上連覺都睡不好.他把做菜當做一種藝術來研究,從白切雞到紅燒肉,從北京烤鴨到廣東點心,他怎麼做怎麼好吃.他能把牛肉炒得跟豆腐一樣嫩,也能把豆腐燒得像魚一樣香.更難得的是還能把每個菜的來歷清清楚楚地說出來.為了把吃的藝術介紹給西方人,去年他花了五個月的工夫,把他多年的做菜心得有條有理地寫成了一本食譜,沒想到一個月就賣了兩萬本.中國菜打進了英國廚房,老黃也意外地出了一陣風頭.有一天他請了幾位朋友去吃中國館子......

DIALOGUE

A: 您來了,幾位啊?請這邊兒坐.您把大衣都給我吧.

B: 我們一共六個人,有沒有大一點兒的桌子?

A: 對不起,大桌子沒有了.您早一點兒來就好了.這樣吧,我把這兩張小桌子給您拼起來怎麼樣?

B: 好吧,六個人坐得下就行.麻煩你先把菜單兒拿來給我們看看.

A: 好,馬上就來.您都請坐,先喝杯茶.

B: 這菜單兒上的菜真不少,我越看越不知道點甚麼好,還是麻煩你介紹幾樣兒你們的拿手菜吧!

A: 我們這兒的家鄉雞,回鍋肉是最拿手的,今天還有剛到的黃魚,來個糖醋黃魚怎麼樣?

B：好啊，這三個菜都要，不過回鍋肉不能太辣，也不能太鹹，做淡一點兒好吧？少放點兒醬油。欸，我記得你們這兒的紅燒豆腐特別好吃，來個紅燒豆腐，再要個素菜——奶油菜花兒有吧？

A：有有有。您幾位喝不喝酒？要不要先來個拼盤兒？

B：我們想喝點兒酒。好，先來個拼盤兒，最後再給我們來個白菜牛肉湯吧，我們都吃米飯。

A：好，好。您這幾位外國朋友是用筷子還是用刀叉？

B：他們幾位筷子用得比我還好，刀叉是用不着的，請你快點兒上菜吧。噢，還有，麻煩你把窗戶關小點兒好嗎？風太大了。

A：拼盤兒來了！

B：來來來，我先敬大家一杯，乾杯啊！請請請，吃菜，吃菜，別客氣，多吃點兒！

（服務員最後把湯拿上來以後，老黃問他：）

B：奇怪啊，今天的糖醋魚怎麼又不甜又不酸？紅燒豆腐也沒有以前那麼香了，你們廚房是不是換了新手？

A：沒有啊！不過我們廚房買了一本新出的食譜，今天的糖醋魚和紅燒豆腐完全是照那個食譜做的。聽說寫那本食譜的是位化學專家，叫黃甚麼白，不知道您認不認⋯⋯

B：不認識！不認識！不認識！

SKETCHES

(1) A：欸，李大姐，甚麼風把你吹來了？真是難得！

B：早就想來看你們，總是沒工夫，你們都好吧？

A：還那樣兒，請坐，請坐！把大衣放在這兒吧，最近忙甚麼啊？

B：我們廠預備把生產拉上去，大家都比以前忙多了。

A：我們公司也沒以前那麼舒服了，為了要把服務搞得更好，一個人常常得做兩個人的事。孩子們都好吧？

B：現在都大了，整天往外跑，學習都很差，我真不知道你怎麼能把孩子教得那麼好。

A：別說了,都一樣.現在的孩子簡直不把父母的話當一回事!欸,餓了吧,我請你去吃鍋貼兒怎麼樣?

B：你怎麼把我當客人了,就在樓下食堂吃碗麵不好嗎?

A：你這麼久不來.當然是客人了.能不能等我幾分鐘?我得先把這件公事拿給老王看看.

B：沒問題,你把應該辦的事都辦完,我多餓一會兒沒關係,到了飯館兒可以多吃一點兒.

(2) A：您怎麼吃這麼少?請再多吃點兒菜!

B：謝謝您,我真的吃飽了.已經比平常多吃了一碗飯,菜太好了!

A：您太客氣了,今天的菜做得都很差.我忙糊塗了.紅燒雞太鹹,回鍋肉太辣,湯裏也忘了放鹽.

B：您別客氣了,我覺得樣樣兒都好,特別是這個糖醋魚館子裏的都沒這麼好吃.

A：要是再做甜一點兒就好了.....我們那邊兒坐吧.您喝咖啡還是喝茶?

B：給我一杯咖啡吧.我飯吃多了,酒也喝多了.

A：您要不要牛奶?放幾塊糖?

B：牛奶不要您給我放兩塊糖吧.....這咖啡真香.....噢,已經十點一刻了,我得走了.

A：您不多坐一會兒了嗎?再喝杯咖啡吧.

B：不了,我得早點兒回去,明天還要上班.謝謝您啊今天真是把您累壞了.

A：哪裏,哪裏.以後有工夫常來玩兒啊!您慢走,不送了,再見!

B：再見!再見!請回!請回!

(1) The 'bǎ' construction

Pattern:　S　A　(neg)　bǎ　　O　　V + other element
　　　　　　他　　　　　　把我的筆拿　走了.

1. 誰把我的茶喝了?

2. 今天太忙了,我把這件事忘了,真對不起.

3. 請你們先把這個問題研究研究,不必馬上做決定.

4. 你能不能把這次去中國的經過跟我們談談?

5. 他們把麻煩都給我了,我把麻煩給誰呢?

6. 你可不可以把你教英文的心得告訴我?

7. 別把筆放在嘴裏,快拿出來!

8. 他想把那一萬本舊書送給圖書館.

9. 我已經把筷子,碗都拿到廚房去了.

10. 我們要搞'四化',不是要搞'西化',你怎麼把'四'字看成'西'字了?

11. 她真能幹,只花了半個小時的工夫就把十個人的飯菜預備好了.

12. 麻煩你拿刀把這塊肉替我切切. (切, 'to cut')

13. 我沒把他當老師,他也沒把我當學生.

14. 他把菜做得太鹹了,我們一邊兒吃,一邊兒喝水.

15. 請你把這個字的用法再給我們解釋一次.

16. 一會兒這樣,一會兒那樣,這個'把'字簡直把我搞糊塗了.

17a. 這兒桌子太多,請你搬兩張出去. (indefinite reference)

　b. 這兒桌子太多,請你把這兩張搬出去. (definite reference)

18a. 這些字我們都寫錯了.

　b. 我們把這些字都寫錯了.

　c. 我們都把這些字寫錯了.

19a. 他把錢拿出來了. ～ 他拿出錢來了.

　b. 我已經把這句話的意思看懂了. ～ 我已經看懂了這句話的意思.

　c. 他把研究歷史的心得寫成了一本書.

20a. 他吃甚麼了?　　他吃糖醋魚了.

　b. 桌子上的菜他都吃了嗎?　　糖醋魚他吃了,紅燒肉他沒吃.

　c. 糖醋魚呢?誰把糖醋魚吃了?　　不是我.

(2) <u>Similarities</u>

(a) Equivalent or not

Patterns: a.　　A　<u>gēn</u>　B　<u>yíyàng</u>/<u>bù yíyàng</u>
　　　　　　你的錶 跟我的 一樣.
　　　　　b.　A　<u>gēn</u>/<u>xiàng</u>　B　<u>yíyàng</u> SV/MV+V
　　　　　　紅燒肉　跟　　糖醋魚 一樣 好吃.

1. 中國畫兒跟英國畫兒很不一樣.
2. ‘思想解放’跟‘解放思想’完全一樣嗎?
3. 西餐的做法跟中餐不一樣吧?
4. 今天的天氣跟昨天一樣好.
5. 這兒的風景像黃山一樣漂亮.
6. 他跟我一樣愛喝酒,我跟他一樣喜歡吃辣的.
7. 你的看法跟他一樣有道理.
8. 我們應該像她一樣把中文學好.
9. 她菜做得跟她母親一樣有名.
10. 他普通話說得快像中國人一樣流利了,進步真快.

(b) On a par with or not

Patterns: a.　　A　(<u>méi</u>)<u>yǒu</u>　B　<u>nàme</u>/<u>zhème</u> SV/MV+V
　　　　　　我 沒(有) 你 那麼 聰明.
　　　　　b.　A　(<u>bú</u>)<u>xiàng</u> B　<u>nàme</u>/<u>zhème</u> SV/MV+V
　　　　　　他 不 像 我 這麼 笨.

1. 你弟弟有你這麼高嗎?　　我們倆差不多一般高.
2. 他的性情不像你這麼急.
3. 她沒有她妹妹那麼活潑,也不像她姐姐那麼愛出風頭.
4. 他一定記得這件事,他沒有我這麼糊塗.
5. 誰敢說這兒的服務沒有那兒好?
6. 中國人不像英國人這麼喜歡喝牛奶.
7. 紅燒肉沒有烤鴨那麼受歡迎.
8. 我菜沒他炒得那麼好,可是他肉切得沒有我這麼快.
9. 她九點半就睡了,不像我們睡得這麼晚.
10. 他寫漢字不像你這麼龍飛鳳舞.

(3) Situational 'de'

1. 北京我沒去過,可是北京烤鴨我倒是吃過的.
2. 他從小吃米飯長大的,三明治是吃不來的.
3. 雖然他說話有點兒糊塗,可是辦事還是有條有理的.
4. 他對化學也是非常有興趣的.
5. 簡單的菜我會炒兩樣,廣東點心我是做不來的.
6. 他太喜歡這張畫兒了,不論多貴,他也要買的.
7. 這個人不專心,不論做甚麼,他總是搞不好的.
8. 他已經快二十了,你把他當做小孩子是不行的.
9. 她來信希望我別去,可是我還是要去的.
10. 如果你不用功,中文是學不好的!

(4) Adverbials marked with 'de'

1. 他整天(地)站在街上,甚麼事也不做.
2. 她整天樓上樓下地跑,累得不得了.
3. 小朋友很活潑地跑出來歡迎我們.
   (cf.小朋友很活潑,跑出來歡迎我們.)
4. 她來晚了,很不好意思地跟老師說:"對不起....."
   (cf.她知道老師說錯了,可是不好意思跟老師說.)
5. 這件公事他大概地看了看,就說沒問題.
   (cf.這件公事他大概已經看過了,你拿走吧.)
6. 他很清楚地把這個人的來歷都告訴我了.
7. 我們很簡單地預備了兩樣菜,想請他來吃頓飯.
8. 聽見外頭有人說中國話,他好奇地走出去看了看.
9. 他非常客氣地問我,能不能把我的拿手菜教給他.
10. 一看見我手上的糖,孩子們都高興地跑過來了.
11. 他買了一塊新錶,把舊的很便宜地賣給他朋友了.
12. 他看見我們,高興地說:"歡迎,歡迎!請進,請進!"
    (cf.他看見我們,高興得說不出話來了.)

(5) Reduplicated stative verbs as adverbials

(a) Monosyllabic SVs

1. 為了這個問題我整整地忙了三天,還是沒搞好.
2. 你得好好兒地學習,要不然考試考不好.
3. 請你快快兒地把這些鍋貼兒拿回廚房去.
4. 搬家的事得慢慢兒地研究,着急也沒用.
5. 你的字寫得太難看了,以後要多多(地)練習.
6. 做這個菜醬油不能太多,少少兒地放一點兒就夠了.
7. 她晚上想去看戲,早早兒地就把晚飯吃了.
8. 他新寫的那本小說在英國很受歡迎,上個月他來倫敦,大大地出了一陣風頭.
9. 你應該好好兒地想想是去還是不去.
10. 他冷冷地說了一句'專家也得好好兒地幹!'就走了.
11. 他把公司的老人慢慢地都換成了他自己的人了.

(b) Disyllabic SVs

1. 吃過午飯,孩子們都高高興興地上公園兒玩兒去了.
2. 我昨天清清楚楚地聽見他說,那件事是他幹的.
3. 別炒菜了,簡簡單單地吃碗麵就行了.
4. 今天晚上舒舒服服地睡一覺,明天就有精神了.
5. 大家客客氣氣地在一起工作,不好嗎?
6. 希望你能有條有理地把這件事的經過寫出來.
7. 你最好實實在在地告訴我們,你是來幹麼的?
8. 這麼冷的天氣,誰不想舒舒服服地在家裏休息?
9. 他信上明明白白地說要給我一萬塊錢,怎麼還不寄來呢?
10. 我們應該實實在在地為人民服務!

(6) Adverbials and predicative complements contrasted

1a. 請你好好兒地寫兩個毛筆字.

  b. 你這兩個毛筆字寫得真好.

2a. 他慢慢兒地把事情都做完了.

  b. 他做事做得很慢.

3a. 那個收音機他們很便宜地賣給我了.

  b. 那個收音機他們賣得很便宜.

4a. 他們很高興地在湖邊兒玩兒了一下午.

  b. 那天下午他們在湖邊兒玩兒得很高興.

5a. 他清清楚楚地把這個問題解釋了一次.

  b. 這個問題他解釋得非常清楚.

(7) Verb constructions that show comparative degree

(a) Complements: V SV yìdiǎnr

1. 請你站近一點兒,看清楚一點兒,那不是倫敦地圖!

2. 對不起,您說得太快了,請您說慢一點兒好嗎?

3. 你的字太小了,我看不清楚,請你寫大一點兒.

4. 上課的時間快到了,走快一點兒吧.(我們走得不夠快.)

5. 這張畫得完全不像,請你畫好一點兒.

6. 今天出去旅行,我們得吃飽一點兒.

7. 這麼熱,請你把窗戶開大點兒.

8. 你做的菜都太淡了,下次能不能請你做鹹一點兒.

9. 一個月不夠,我希望能在中國住久一點兒.

10. 請你把這個東西放高點兒,找個孩子拿不到的地方.

(b) Adverbials: SV yìdiǎnr V (SVs being kuài, màn, zǎo, wǎn)

1. 要下雨了,快點兒跑吧!(a.馬上開始跑. b.=跑快點兒吧.)

2. 你慢點兒給錢,先看看東西好不好.

3. 麵已經冷了,快點兒吃吧.(a.馬上開始吃. b.=吃快點兒吧.)

4. 快點兒出去看看誰來了.

5. 明天請你早一點兒來. (= 來早一點兒.)

6. 我得先去醫院看個朋友,晚一刻鐘到,行不行?

7. 早點兒開始可以早點兒做完.

8. 照他的說法,還是晚點兒結婚好. (= 結婚晚點兒好.)

(c) SV V yìdiǎnr/NU M N (SVs: duō, shǎo, zǎo, wǎn)

1. 沒甚麼好菜,可是請您多吃點兒.

2. 四塊錢是少一點兒,多給他一塊吧.

3. 你還有那麼多事沒做完呢,少看點兒電視吧.

4. 我知道你有道理,不過還是請你少說兩句.

5. 大夫說我應該多吃點兒素菜,少吃點兒肉.

6. 我太胖了,咖啡裏得少放點兒糖. (or: 少放一塊糖.)

7. 我敬你,多喝點兒啊!你看,我已經乾了三杯了,你還是那一杯.

8. 今天的牛肉我多炒了兩分鐘,不夠嫩了.

9. 明天請你們早來五分鐘,可以嗎?

10. 我們的車晚到了一刻鐘.

(8) Correlative clause

Patterns: a.　yuè...yuè...
　　　　他越說越快;越快我越聽不懂.
　　　b.　yuè lai yuè ...
　　　　他越來越糊塗了.
　　　c.　búlùn QW　　　yě/dōu/háishi ...
　　　　不論多冷他　都　　　不買大衣.

1. 中文越學越有意思,越有意思我就越想學.

2. 點菜真不容易,這個菜單我越看越糊塗.

3. 錢是越多越好,工作是越少越好.

4. 新手都一樣,越怕搞錯,越容易錯.

5. 房子越住越小,汽車越坐越大.

6. 東西越來越貴,工作越來越難找.

7. 電腦越來越進步,人的腦子也就越來越沒用.
8. 風越來越大,街上的人也越來越少,我心裏也就越來越着急.
9. 喝咖啡的人越來越多,喝茶的人越來越少.
10. 不論你多忙,今天也得把這件公事辦完.
11. 不論你給他多少錢,他也不幹這種事.
12. 不論他說得多好聽,我還是不想跟他去.
13. 不論你喜不喜歡都得照他的法子辦事.
14. 不論你是誰,晚上十點以後我是不見客人的.
15. 不論換甚麼人來教他,他也學不好.

(9) Causative verbs

1. 客人都到了,可以上菜了.
2. 今天館子人多,上菜上得真慢.
3. 中國南方出米,所以南方人都吃米飯.
4. 他希望每年能出一本書.
5. 說話的人很多,可是出錢的人很少.
6. 給我們來四十個鍋貼兒,一大碗酸辣湯.
7. 麻煩你,再來點兒茶!
8. 這麼多人,我得下多少斤麵啊? (下麵,'cook (lit. 'lower') noodles')

室	shì　* room 辦公室 office	擺	bǎi　　　[摆] (V) to put, to place, to 　　arrange, to display
着	zhe　　　[着] (V suffix) indicating contin- ued state or action	綠	lǜ　　　[绿] (SV) green
套	tào (N) sheath, case, cover (V) to sheathe, to cover with (M) set, suit, suite	灰	huī (N) ashes; dust (SV) grey
沙	shā (N) sand (SV) (of voice) hoarse 沙發 sofa, settee	缸	gāng (N) vat, jar, mug, bowl
立	lì * to be standing (V) to set up	髮	fà　　*　[发] hair (on the human head)頭髮
排	pái (V) to arrange (in a row); to 　　line up 排隊 (M) row, line; platoon	鏡	jìng　　*　[镜] mirror 鏡子; lens 眼鏡兒 eye-glasses
架	jià * frame; rack; shelf (M) for machines, aeroplanes, 　　etc.	穿	chuān (V) to pierce through; to 　　pass through; to put on 　　(clothes, footwear)
牆	qiáng　　　[墙] (N) wall　　　　(M:面,道)	貿	mào　　*　[贸] to trade 貿易
掛	guà　　　[挂] (V) to hang, to suspend; to 　　ring off (M) a string (of things)	曆	lì　　*　[历] calendar 月曆 monthly calendar
遠	yuǎn　　　[远] (SV) far, distant, remote	里	lǐ * lane, square (in place names) (M) 1 里 里 = ½ km 公里
顏	yán '顏' *　[颜] face; countenance; colour a surname	漸	jiàn　　*　[渐] gradual(ly), by degrees
色	sè　　　* colour 顏色; look	黑	hēi (SV) black; dark

低	dī (低) (SV) low (V) to let droop, to lower (the head)	喂	wéi, wèi (I) Hello! (in telephoning); Hey!
屋	wū　　　　　* house; room 屋子　　(M:間)	雪	xuě (雪) (N) snow 下雪 to snow
隔	gé (隔) (V) to separate, partition (CV) at a distance from; after or at an interval of	度	dù * standard; measure; degree of intensity (M) degree; occasion
緊	jǐn　　　　　[紧] (SV) tight, tense; strict; urgent; hard up	故	gù　　　　　* old; deceased; cause (LC) therefore 故事 story
輕	qīng　　　　[轻] (SV) light; gentle 年輕 young	宮	gōng　　　　[宫] (N) palace; hall
槍	qiāng '鎗'　　[枪] (N) spear; rifle; pistol (M:枝)	偉	wěi　　*　　[伟] big; great; heroic
匹	pǐ (M) for horses, mules; a bolt of cloth	繫	xì　　　　　[系] (V) to tie, to fasten; to relate to
切	qiè　　　　　* be close to; be anxious to; be sure to 一切 all, every(thing)	幫	bāng　　　　[帮] (V) to help (N/M) clique, gang, group 四人幫 the Gang of Four
鈴	líng　　　　　[铃] (N) small bell	處	chù　　　　　[处] * place, locality (M) department; office
響	xiǎng (響)　　[响] (V) to sound, to make a sound (SV) loud, noisy	設	shè　　　　　[设] (V) to set up, to establish
趕	gǎn　　　　　[赶] (V) to hurry; to catch up with; to drive (a cart); to drive away	續	xù　　*　　　[续] to continue; to extend 手續 procedures, formal- ities
途	tú　　*　　　[途] way, road, route 長途 long-distance	費	fèi　　　　　[费] * fee; expenses, charge (V) to spend (money or time) a surname
線	xiàn '綫'　　[线] (N) thread; wire; line	鎊	bàng　　　　[镑] (M) pound (sterling)

病 bìng
(SV) to be ill 病了，有病
(N) illness, disease; defect

STROKE-ORDER

室　宀　空　室　[宀]
着　兰　半　芏　羊　着 (着)　兰　芏　着　[目]
套　大　太　车　查　奎　套　[大]
沙　氵　沙　沙　[水]
立　亠　六　立　[立]
排　扌　扚　扚　扚　排　[手扌]
架　力　加　架　[木]
牆 (墙)　乚　爿　爿　爿　牁　牂　牆　牆　土　圠　圵　坧　墙　墙　墙　[爿]
掛　扌　扜　挂　掛 (挂)　[手扌]
遠　土　吉　吉　袁　遠 (远)　[辵]
顏　立　产　彦　顔　顏 (颜)　[頁]
色　ク　刍　夅　色　[色]
擺　扌　押　擇　擺 (摆)　[手扌]
綠　糸　糹　約　綵　綠 (绿)　[糸]
灰　一　广　厂　灰　灰　灰　[火]
缸　亠　二　午　击　击　缸　[缶]
髮　長　髟　髟　髥　髮　髮　[髟]
(发)　乚　少　戈　发　发　[广]
鏡　金　鈩　鏡　鏡 (镜)　[金]
穿　宀　穴　空　空　穿　穿　[穴]
貿　丶　ム　ム　卯　貿 (贸)　[貝]
曆　厂　厤　麻　曆 (历)　[日]
里　口　曰　日　旦　甲　里　[里]
漸　氵　浐　漸　漸 (渐)　[水氵]

黑　口　四　罒　甲　里　黑　[黑]
低　亻　仃　仾　低　低　[人亻]
屋　尸　屋　屋　[尸]
隔　阝　阿　隔　隔　隔　[阜阝]
緊　丂　臣　臤　緊 (紧)　[糸]
輕　車　軣　輕 (轻)　车　�　軽　轻　[車]
槍　木　栌　柃　槍　槍　槍 (枪)　柃　枪　[木]
匹　一　匚　兀　匹　[匸]
切　一　七　切　切　[刀]
鈴　金　釸　鈴 (铃)　[金]
響　纟　鄉　鄉　響 (响)　[音]
趕　走　赳　赳　趕 (赶)　[走]
途　人　今　余　途　[辵]
線　糸　絼　線 (线)　纟　线　线　线　[糸]
喂　口　吧　呷　喂　喂　喂　[口]
雪　二　干　雫　雪　雪　雪　[雨]
度　广　广　庐　庐　度　[广]
故　十　古　故　[攴攵]
宮　宀　宁　宀　宮 (宫)　[宀]
偉　亻　亻　仁　仲　倍　偉　偉　[人亻]
(伟)　亻　仁　纬　伟　[伟]
繫　車　車　毄　繫 (系)　[糸]
幫　圭　封　幇 (帮)　三　丰　邦　帮　[巾]
處　卜　上　广　庐　虏　虍　處 (处)　[虍]
設　言　訉　設　[言]

159

續 糹 糹 績續 (续) 纩续续 [糸]   鏽 金 鈋 鏟鏟鏽 (锈)   [金]
費 フ コ 弗 費 費 (费)   [贝]   病 亠 广 疒 病病   [疒]

VOCABULARY

間　jiān (M) for rooms

辦公室　bàngōngshì (N) office

着　-zhe (V suffix) durative suffix

套　tào (M) set, suit, suite

沙發　shāfā (N) sofa; easy chair

立　lì (V) stand; set up, establish

排　pái (M) a row of
　　　(V) form a row

書架　shūjià (N) bookshelf

面　miàn (N) face, surface, side
　　　(M) for walls

牆　qiáng (N) wall

掛　guà (V) hang

好幾　hǎo jǐ (A NU) a good few —

山水(畫兒)　shānshuǐ(huàr) (N)
　　　landscape (paintings)

離　lí (CV) separated from

遠　yuǎn (SV) far, distant

辦公桌　bàngōngzhuō (N) (office)
　　　desk

顏色　yánsè (N) colour

電話　diànhuà (N) telephone

擺　bǎi (V) place, lay out, display

綠(色)　lǜ(se) (SV) green (coloured)

烟灰缸　yānhuīgāng (N) ashtray

頭髮　tóufa (N) hair (on head)

灰白　huībái (SV) grey-white

眼鏡兒　yǎnjìngr (N) spectacles

穿　chuān (V) wear, put on (of
　　　garments)

西服　xīfú (N) Western clothes; suit

中年人　zhōngnián rén (N) middle-aged
　　　person

貿易　màoyì (N) trade

總經理　zǒngjīnglǐ (N) general mana-
　　　ger

總　zǒng (AT) general, chief, head;
　　　overall

對面　duìmian (PW) opposite

月曆　yuèlì (N) monthly calendar

在　zài (CV) engaged in, in the pro-
　　　cess of

算日子　suàn rìzi (VO) reckon up the
　　　days; work out what
　　　day it is

日子 rìzi (N) day, date, special day

萬里長城　Wànlǐ Chángchéng (PW) the
　　　Great Wall

里　lǐ (M) 1 里 = ½ km

　　　(公里 gōnglǐ, 'km';
　　　英里 yīnglǐ, 'mile')

正　zhèng (A) just then, just at that
　　　point

毛毛雨　máomáoyǔ (N) drizzle

漸漸(地) jiànjiàn(de) (A) gradually

黑　hēi (SV) black; dark

-下來　-xialai (V/SV comp) down, to a
　　　halt, increasingly, etc

低　dī (SV) low
　　　(V) droop

屋子　wūzi (N) room

160

來回來去(地) láihuí láiqù(de) (A) backwards and forwards

起來 -qilai (V/SV comp) begin, come to, etc.

每隔 měigé (CV) at intervals of; every (so often)

隔 gé (V) isolate, separate, cut off

正在 zhèngzài (A) just ——ing

要緊 yàojǐn (SV) important, urgent

自從 zìcóng (CV) ever since

年輕人 niánqīng rén (N) young person

單槍匹馬 dānqiāng-pǐmǎ (set phrase) 'single spear one horse': singlehanded

槍 qiāng (N) spear; gun

電報 diànbào (N) telegram

會 huì (MV) would, be sure to; be likely to

報告 bàogào (V/N) report

一切 yíqiè (N) everything; all, every

從...起 cóng ... qǐ starting from ...

緊張 jǐnzhāng (SV) tense, tight, nervous; in short supply

鈴 líng (N) small bell

響 xiǎng (V) sound (SV) loud

趕緊 gǎnjǐn (A) hurriedly

長途 chángtú (AT) long-distance

線 xiàn (N) line, wire, thread

接通 jiētōng (V) connect, put through

喂 wéi, wèi (I) hello! hey!

雪 xuě (N) snow

下雪 xià-xuě (V-O) to snow

零下 língxià (PW) below zero

度 dù (M) degree

故宮 Gùgōng (PW) (former palace) the Palace Museum

旅館 lǚguǎn (N) hotel

偉大 wěidà (SV) great, imposing, mighty

進行 jìnxíng (V) go on, be under way; carry on, carry out

方面 fāngmiàn (N) aspect, respect, side, quarter

聯繫 liánxì (V) get in contact with (N) contact, link

有關 yǒu-guān (SV) relevant, (the one) concerned

幫忙 bāng-máng (V) help

設立 shèlì (V) set up, establish

辦事處 bànshìchù (N) bureau

下去 -xiaqu (V/SV comp) continue, carry on

手續 shǒuxù (N) procedures, formality

旅費 lǚfèi (N) travel expenses

鎊 bàng (M) pound (sterling)

毛病 máobìng (N) fault, defect, shortcomings

病 bìng (N) illness

出毛病 chū máobìng (VO) develop a fault

排隊 pái-duì (V-O) line up, queue up

電影院 diànyǐngyuàn (PW) cinema

盤子 pánzi (N) plate, tray

161

　　這是一間相當大的辦公室,一進門左邊兒放着一套沙發,右邊兒立着一排書架,四面牆上掛着好幾幅中國山水,離窗戶不遠有一張辦公桌,上頭除了兩個顏色不同的電話以外,只擺着一個綠色的大烟灰缸,桌子後頭坐着一位頭髮灰白,戴着眼鏡兒,穿着西服的中年人,他就是這家華僑貿易公司的錢總經理,這時候他一邊兒抽着烟,一邊兒看着對面牆上的月曆,不知道他是在算日子還是在看月曆上的那幅萬里長城,窗外正下着毛毛雨,天漸漸地黑下來了,錢總經理抽完烟,站起來把燈開開以後就低着頭在屋子裏來回來去地走起來了,可是每隔兩三分鐘,他的眼睛就要看看桌兒上的電話,對了,他正在等一個非常要緊的電話,自從公司的小萬去中國以後,他天天都在着急,不知道這位平常愛玩兒的年輕人單槍匹馬能不能把事情辦好,昨天接到他的電報說一、兩天就會打電話回來,報告一切,所以今天從早晨起錢總經理就一直在緊張地等着……

　　忽然電話鈴響了,他趕緊跑過去接,果然是小萬來的長途電話,線接通了以後:

DIALOGUE

A: 喂!總經理嗎? 我是萬通啊!

B: 喂! 小萬嗎? 我正在等你的電話呢! 北京怎麼樣啊?

A: 冷得不得了,現在正在下大雪呢,零下十二度!

B: 一切都沒問題吧?

A: 沒問題!冷是冷,風景可是真漂亮,故宮,北海離我住的旅館都不遠,我已經去過好幾次了,真是不到北京不知道中國的偉大!

B: 我是問你公司的事情有沒有問題,你怎麼談起風景來了?

A: 噢!公司的事情啊?還在進行呢,各方面都聯繫得差不多了,有關單位都很幫忙,看起來是不會有甚麼問題的。

B: 那就好!喂,小萬,在北京設立辦事處的事有希望嗎?

A: 有是有,不過現在北京房子相當緊張,找起來很不容易,恐怕還得多等些時候。

B: 可是一直等下去也不是辦法啊!喂,你打算甚麼時候去上海?

A: 我正在辦手續呢,這兒的事一完,馬上就飛上海,噢,對了,總經理,有一件事得請您幫忙。

B: 甚麼事啊?你說吧!

A: 我的旅費差不多快用完了,公司能不能先借給我五百鎊?

B: 喂,你說甚麼?我聽不清楚啊!

A: 我說我的旅費快用完了,想跟公司借五百鎊。

B: 喂喂,你說甚麼?我一句都聽不清楚,大概是線出毛病了,小萬,下次再談吧!

SKETCHES

(1) A: 喂,景山公司嗎?

B: 找誰啊?

A: 小黃在嗎?

B: 我就是,你哪位?

A: 聽不出來啊?你猜猜吧!

B: 欸,我正忙着呢,沒工夫跟你猜着玩兒,找我有甚麼事嗎?

A: 沒事就不能找你了?好,跟你說吧,我上午排了半天隊才搞到兩張票,明天晚上想不想看電影兒?

B: 好啊,我明天晚上正好沒事兒,在哪兒啊?

A: 就在離我們廠不遠的那個電影院,七點鐘老地方見吧.

B: 喂,喂,等一等,我還沒搞清楚你是誰呢.

A: 甚麼?你真不知道我是誰啊?小黃,你再想想上星期天.....

B: 小黃?我不是小黃,我姓王,我們這兒連半個姓黃的都沒有.

A: 你們不是景山公司嗎?

B: 不是,我們這兒是青山公司,你打錯了!

A: 打錯了?!那.....你為甚麼要接呢?

(2)　　離現在已經有兩千多年了,有一天在中國北方離海邊兒不遠的一條路上,有人聽見兩個小孩兒正在談有關太陽的問題:

A: 欸,我忽然想起一個問題來:你說太陽甚麼時候離我們最近?

B: 當然早晨離我們最近.

A: 為甚麼呢?

B: 你看早晨太陽剛出來的時候多麼大,慢慢兒地越來越小,到了中午只有盤子那麼大了.東西離我們越遠,看起來就越小,這不是很簡單嗎?!

A: 我看不完全對吧?

B: 為甚麼呢?

A: 你看早晨太陽出來的時候,我們一點兒也不覺得熱,可是到了中午就熱起來了,平常不是離火越近越覺得熱嗎?所以我說我們中午離太陽最近.

SPEECH PATTERNS

(1) The progressive aspect

(a) Sentence particle ne

1. 他在屋子裏幹麽呢?　　打電話呢.
2. 你弟弟呢?　　在樓上睡覺呢.
3. 他們倆做甚麽呢?　　看小説呢.
4. 老李怎麽還沒來?　　他在街上買東西呢.

(b) Zhèng ... (ne)

1. 我們正説他呢,他就來了.
2. 他們正吃飯呢,我們在外頭等一會兒吧.
3. 我進門的時候,牆上的鐘正打十二點呢.
4. 雨正大呢,吃了飯再走吧.
5. 今天早晨我正走過文化宮門口的時候,聽見後頭有人叫我...
6. 我正急得不知道怎麽辦的時候,電話鈴響了.
7. 老李呢?　　快去,快去,他正在辦公室等你呢!
8. 那些學生正在那兒談天説地呢!

(c) Zài ... (ne)

1. 最近很多人都在談年輕人抽烟的問題.
2. 我在跟你説話,你聽見了沒有?　　甚麽?你説甚麽?
3. 他這些年一直在研究為甚麽吃中國菜不容易胖.
4. 風在吹,雨在下,我甚麽時候才能回家?
5. 我剛才還在説不要紅的,你怎麽又給了我一個紅的?
6. 你在忙甚麽?　　我天天都在作報告,一個完了,又來一個.
7. 他每天都在為三頓飯着急,總是在打算怎麽跟人借錢.
8. 他沒(有)在學習,他在看電視呢.
9. 她不是在寫字,是在畫畫兒.

165

(d) <u>Zhèngzài</u> ... (<u>ne</u>)

1. 我們進辦公室的時候,他正在打電話呢.
2. 去中國教書的事有希望嗎? 正在進行呢.
3. 你正在幹麼呢?能不能來幫幫忙?
   我正在寫一封很要緊的信,寫完了就來.
4. 喂,總機,接通了沒有? 您別着急,正在給您接呢.(總機,
   'exchange')
5. 這兩天他怎麼這麼用功? 他正在預備考試呢.
6. 他是不是正在辦公呢? 沒有,他正在跟朋友打牌呢.
7. 你正在忙嗎? 沒有,正在休息呢.
8. 我進來的時候你正在跟誰說話?
   我沒跟誰說話,我正在練習第十六課的對話呢.(對話, 'dialogue')

(2) The continuous aspect

(a) Main verb with <u>-zhe</u>

1. 老王幹麼呢? 他在沙發上坐着呢.
2. 他手上拿着甚麼呢? 我也看不清楚,好像是一把手槍.
3. 要不要我跟你一塊兒進去? 不必了,你就在這兒等着我吧.
4. 你朋友找着房子了嗎? 還沒呢,還在旅館住着呢.
5. 別老低着頭!看着我!
6. 別站着,快坐下來,後頭的人要說話了.
7. 裏頭說着話呢,你在外頭等幾分鐘吧.
8. 你別老坐着,每隔半小時應該站起來走走.
9. 他心裏一直在想着錢的問題.
10. 你一個人去得帶着槍吧!

(b) V-<u>zhe</u> indicating a settled state that results from the original action of the verb

1. 沙發上坐着兩個人,一胖一瘦,都戴着眼鏡兒.
2. 辦公桌上放着不少東西,就是沒有烟灰缸.
3. 你快出去看看,門外頭站着一個中年人,說是要找你.

166

4. 這簡直不像一間辦公室,窗户上貼着舊報,牆上掛着前年的月曆.
5. 桌子中間放着一個大碗,碗上畫着一條長龍.
6. 這間屋子裏一共住着多少人?
7. 這麼冷,快把窗户關上吧! 窗户本來就是關着的,沒開着.
8. 你看旅館門口的地上寫着四個大白字,'不准 —— 甚麼?'

(c) V/SV-_zhe_ used in a subordinate role

1. 你說怎麼去? 路不遠,走着去吧.
2. 這件事我一個人做不了,你得幫着我做. 好,沒問題.
3. 她正在做飯吧? 沒有,你看她在那兒坐着看報呢.
4. 你吃完再說吧,吃着東西說話,不太好看.
5. 街上汽車這麼多,你不能低着頭走路.
6. 媽說不准吃着飯看書,你不知道嗎?
   我沒有吃着飯看書,我看着書吃飯也不行嗎?
7. 你怎麼一個人關着門喝酒,朋友都不要了?
8. 忙甚麼呢? 我正忙着跟各方面聯繫呢.
9. 他怎麼只吃了一口飯就跑了? 他急着要到火車站去接朋友.
10. 她一發現說錯了話,馬上就紅着臉跑出去了.
11. 母親拉着孩子的手說:"別怕,你一定可以做好的!"
12. 我們幾個人一邊兒走着,一邊兒說着,很快就到了.
13. 抽着烟,喝着酒,大家高興極了.
14. 他一邊兒跑着,一邊兒叫着,街上的人都在看他.
15. 她一邊兒跟我說着話,一邊兒就把菜炒好了.

(3) **Distance**

Patterns: a.   A   lí   B   yuǎn/jìn
           他家 離 公司 遠不遠?
        b.   A   lí   B   (yǒu) NU M (lù/dì)
           倫敦 離 北京 有 幾千公里?
        c.   A   lí   B   yǒu NU M N
           現在 離 上班時間還 有 三分鐘.

1. 辦公室離家遠嗎？　　很近，我就住在辦公室的樓上。
2. 故宮離這兒有多遠？　　不遠，從這兒往東一直走，十分鐘就到。
3. 你住的旅館在哪兒？　　在城外，離這兒最少有八公里。
4. 他家離車站比我家離車站大概遠半英里。
5. 她住的地方離北海公園只有幾分鐘的路。
6. 我們公社離南京大概有三百里地。
7. 那件事離現在有多久了？　　已經有七、八年了吧，沒人記得了。
8. 快下課了吧？　　下課？現在才十點半，離下課還有二十分鐘呢。

(4) <u>Extended use of directional complements</u>

Patterns: a. 我們正在路上的時候，忽然下起雪來了。(start to)
b. 他們工廠的辦事處已經辦起來了。(in operation)
c. 這個問題研究起來非常有意思。(when you come to)
d. 中文越來越難，我實在學不下去了。(carry on)
e. 這是誰唱的歌兒，你聽出來了嗎？(detect)
f. 火車快到站了，你看已經慢下來了。(progressive)

1. 奇怪，今天又冷起來了，多少度啊？
2. 快考試了，學生都緊張起來了。
3. 我們一說他正在搞對象，他的臉馬上就紅起來了。
4. 線還沒接通，他就說起話來了。
5. 別人還沒吃完飯，他就抽起烟來了。
6. 他真能幹，一個人就把辦事處搞起來了。
7. 忘了自己的電話多少號?! 你再想想！
　　啊，我想起來了，四四 七三二六。
8. 他們把那個地方隔起來了，不准人進去。(隔起來，'set apart, cordon off')
9. 這件事啊，說起來容易，做起來難。
10. 他弟弟看起來很聰明，可是念起書來笨得跟牛一樣。
11. 算起來，我已經有三年沒吃過中國飯了。
12. 比起他們來我差遠了。　　你別客氣了！

13. 看起來天氣還要冷下去.
14. 走吧,別聽了!再聽下去我就要睡着了. 我已經睡了一覺了.
15. 她一看見老師來了,緊張得說不下去了.
16. 信寄不到,電話打不通,誰能想出辦法來?
17. 他穿着西服,戴着太陽眼鏡兒,我沒認出他來.
18. 我花了三天的工夫才把這個報告寫出來.
19. 天漸漸黑下來了,路上的車也越來越少了.
20. 他已經把經理的工作接下來了.

(5) The concessive form of 'X shi X'

Pattern: 這張山水畫兒不錯吧? 不錯是不錯,就是太貴了.

1. 你單槍匹馬一個人去,不怕嗎? 怕是怕,可是不去不行.
2. 這種電視機太貴了! 貴是貴一點兒,可是東西實在好.
3. 你還學不學? 學是學,不過想換個地方.
4. 你想到中國去旅行嗎? 想是想,可是沒人給我出旅費.
5. 你不買了嗎? 我買還是要買,不過不買這種顏色的.
6. 你給他打電話了嗎? 打是打了,不過沒打通.
7. 她去過上海嗎?
   去是去過,不過那時候她才三個月,甚麼都不知道.
8. 你沒帶着槍嗎? 帶是帶着呢,可是不知道怎麼用.

(6) The modal verb 'hui'

1. 你看今天會不會下雨? 大概不會吧.
2. 這件事一定是他幹的!
   不會的,他那麼聰明的人,不會幹這種笨事.
3. 我真不明白,他怎麼會連北京的'京'字都不會寫!
4. 看起來雪不會很快就停的.
5. 如果你不照着我的話做就一定會出毛病.
6. 他不高興,不會是因為我沒借錢給他吧.

列	liè (V) to list (M) a row of	讓	ràng [让] (V) to yield; to allow (CV) by (in passive construc- tions)
奔	bēn (LC) to run, to rush (V) to go to, to be bound for	涼	liáng [凉] (SV) cool, cold 涼快 pleasantly cool (of weather)
夜	yè 亱 * night (M) a night	爽	shuǎng (SV) crisp, refreshing
河	hé (N) river (M:條)	秋	qiū * autumn 秋天
無	wú [无] (LC) not to have; there is not; without (AT) -less	踪	zōng 蹤 * footprint, trace, tracks
際	jì * [际] border, boundary, edge; interval; between; occasion 國際 international	言	yán * speech; word 語言 language
藍	lán [蓝] (SV) blue a surname	播	bō (V) to sow (seeds); to spread; to broadcast
空	kōng * sky 天空; air 空氣 (SV) empty, hollow, void	醒	xǐng (V) to awake; to regain con- sciousness; to sober up
被	bèi (CV) by (in passive construc- tions) (N) quilt	闊	kuò 濶 [阔] * wide (SV) rich, ostentatious
洗	xǐ (V) to wash; to develop (photographs); to shuffle (cards)	吸	xī (V) to inhale; to absorb 吸烟 = 抽烟
淨	jìng 净 [净] * clean 乾淨 (A) merely; nothing but	引	yǐn (V) to draw; to lead; to attract
悶	mēn [闷] (SV) stuffy, close	相	xiàng (N) looks, appearance; phys- iognomy 照相 to take photographs

尋	xún * [寻] to look for, to search for	攔	lán [拦] (V) to bar, to block, to hold back

物	wù *
	(LC) thing (an object or
	    article); substance
		代	dài
			(V) to substitute for; to
			    take the place of
			(CV) for

騾	luó * [骡] mule 騾子 (M: 匹) 騾馬 mules and horses	表	biǎo * surface; to show, to ex- press; -meter (N) a table, list, form
勞	láo * [劳] toil, labour; tired; to trouble a surname	興	xīng [兴] * to prosper, to rise, to start (V) to become popular
動	dòng [动] (V) to move; to use; to start 勞動 to work, labour(ing)	奮	fèn * [奋] to exert oneself, to put forth effort
留	liú (V) to retain, to keep, to remain 留學 study abroad	汗	hàn (N) sweat, perspiration 出汗 (V-O) to sweat

提	tí
	(V) to lift (from above), to
	    carry; to mention; to
	    propose
		港	gǎng
			(N) harbour, port
			香港 Hong Kong

土	tǔ (N) earth, soil, dust (AT) local (SV) uncouth	護	hù [护] (V) to protect 護照 passport
驗	yàn [验] (V) to examine, to test 經驗 (N/V) experience	偷	tōu (V) to steal 小偷(兒) petty thief
億	yì [亿] (NU) hundred million 億萬 hundreds of millions	廁	cè * [厕] lavatory 廁所 男廁(所) Gents 女廁(所) Ladies
終	zhōng * [终] end, finish	誤	wù * [误] error, erroneous; to miss (a train, etc.); by mistake
於	yú * [于] (LC) at, in; in regard to 終於 at (long) last	託	tuō [托] (V) to entrust; to ask sb. to do sth. for one
臺	tái [台] (N) terrace, raised platform, stage short for Taiwan 臺灣	箱	xiāng * chest, box, case (M) chest/box/trunk of

冬	dōng * winter 冬天	頤	yí * [颐] cheek; to nourish 頤和園 the Summer Palace (outside Peking)
衞	wèi '衞' * [卫] to defend, to guard, to protect 衞生 hygiene a surname	座	zuò * seat 座位 ; pedestal (M) for mountains, bridges, buildings, etc.
紙	zhǐ [纸] (N) paper (M:張)	橋	qiáo [桥] (N) bridge (M:座)
打	dá (M) dozen (transliteration)	孔	kǒng (N) hole, aperture a surname 孔子 Confucius

STROKE-ORDER

列	一 厂 歹 歹 列	[刀]	播	扌 扩 扩 扩 护 拌 採 播	[手]
奔	大 本 李 奔	[大]	醒	酉 醒	[酉]
夜	一 广 疒 疒 夜	[夕]	閣	門 閣 (阁)	[門]
河	氵 氵 河 河	[水]	吸	口 叮 叨 吸	[口]
無	一 二 午 無 無 無 (无)	[火]	引	丁 弓 弓 引	[弓]
際	阝 阝 阝 阝 阝 際 (际)	[阜]	相	木 相	[目]
藍	艹 艹 芝 芝 莊 藍 藍 (蓝)	[艸]	尋	丁 ヲ ヨ 彐 尹 尋 (寻)	[寸]
空	宀 穴 空	[穴]	物	丷 牛 牛 物 物	[牛]
被	衤 衤 衤 袥 被 被	[衣]	驟	馬 馭 驟 (骤)	[馬]
洗	氵 洪 洗	[水]	勞	火 炒 燃 勞 (劳)	[力]
淨	氵 氵 氵 沪 沪 渭 淨 淨 (净)	[水]	動	一 台 台 重 重 動 (动)	[力]
悶	門 悶 (闷)	[心]	留	匚 卯 卯 留	[田]
讓	言 訁 詝 謹 謹 讓 讓 (让)	[言]	提	扌 押 提	[手]
涼	氵 氵 涼 (凉)	[水]	土	十 土	[土]
爽	厂 厂 爽 爽 爽 爽	[爻]	驗	馬 馭 駘 騐 驗 (验)	[馬]
秋	禾 秋	[禾]	億	亻 仟 偣 億 (亿)	[人]
踪	口 卫 凡 足 踪 踪	[足]	終	糸 終 終 終 (终)	[糸]
言	言	[言]	於	方 扩 於 (于)	[方]

172

臺　　士　吉　吉　臺　臺　(台)　　　　　[至]　　　託　　言　訐　託　(托)　　　　　　[言]
攔　　扌　捫　捫　欄　攔　攔　(拦)　[手]　　　箱　　艹　笨　箱　　　　　　　　　　[竹]
代　　亻　仁　代　代　　　　　　　　　[人]　　　冬　　夂　夂　冬　　　　　　　　　　[冫]
表　　二　丰　主　丯　耒　表　表　[衣]　　　衛　　彳　彳　卫　律　律　衛　(卫)　[行]
奮　　大　奞　奮　(奋)　　　　　　　　[大]　　　紙　　糸　絍　紵　紙　(纸)　　　　[糸]
汗　　氵　汗　　　　　　　　　　　　　[水]　　　打　　扌　打　　　　　　　　　　　　[手]
港　　氵　汇　沪　洪　洪　港　港　[水]　　　頤　　丆　匠　丐　臣　頤　(颐)　　[頁]
護　　言　討　諽　護　(护)　　　　　　[言]　　　座　　宀　广　庀　座　座　　　　　　[广]
偷　　亻　介　价　俞　偷　　　　　　　[人]　　　橋　　木　杧　柞　椿　橋　橋　(桥)　[木]
廁　　一　广　庿　廁　(厕)　　　　　　[广]　　　孔　　乛　了　孑　孔　　　　　　　　[子]
誤　　言　訐　訝　訳　誤　(误)　　　[言]

VOCABULARY

天亮　tiānliàng (S-Predicate) day-
　　　　break (lit: sky bright)

列車　lièchē (N) train (rail-
　　　　way term)

奔　bēn (V) rush, speed

(黑)夜　(hēi)yè (N) (dark) night

黃河　Huánghé (PR) Yellow River

車窗　chēchuāng (N) carriage win-
　　　　dow

望　wàng (V) look into the distance,
　　　look across at

南方　nánfāng (PW) the south

青山綠水　qīngshān lùshuǐ (set
　　　phrase) verdant hills and
　　　green waters

眼前　yǎnqián (PW) before the eyes

一望無際　yí wàng wújì (set
　　　phrase) 'look afar no bound'
　　　— as far as the eye can see

華北平原　Huáběi Píngyuán (PW)
　　　North China Plain

藍(色)　lán(sè) (SV) blue (coloured)

天空　tiānkōng (N) sky

被　bèi (CV) by (in passive con-
　　　structions)

洗　xǐ (V) wash

明淨　míngjìng (SV) bright and
　　　clean, luminous

悶熱　mēnrè (SV/N) sultry; sultriness

讓　ràng (V) let, allow
　　　(CV) by (in passive con-
　　　structions)

涼爽　liángshuǎng (SV) cool and
　　　refreshing

秋風　qiūfēng (N) autumn wind (=
　　　秋天的風　)

無影無踪　wúyǐng wúzōng (set
　　　phrase) without shadow with-
　　　out trace

北京語言學院　Běijīng Yǔyán Xué-
　　　yuàn (PR) Peking Languages
　　　Institute

同車　tóngchē (N) 'same car': fellow
　　　(of travellers)

旅客　lǚkè (N) traveller, passenger

清早　qīngzǎo (TW) early morning

廣播 guǎngbo (N/V) broadcast

醒 xǐng (V) awake(n)

  叫醒 jiàoxǐng (V) 'call awake' wake up

立刻 lìkè (A) immediately

開闊 kāikuò (SV) wide, open (of spaces)

景色 jǐngsè (N) landscape, scenery, scene

吸引 xīyǐn (V) attract, draw

照相 zhào xiàng (VO) take photograph

  照相機 zhàoxiàngjī (N) camera

更是 gèngshi (A) further, on top of that

不停地 bùtíngde (A) unceasingly

尋找 xúnzhǎo (V) seek, look for

鏡頭 jìngtóu (N) shot (photography); camera lens

地裏 dì-lǐ (PW) in the fields

農作物 nóngzuòwù (N) farm crops

騾馬大車 luó-mǎ dàchē (adjunct + N) mule and horse carts

勞動 láodòng (V/N) labour (physical)

社員 shèyuán (N) member of a shè (society, association, commune)

照下來 zhàoxialai (V) get on film

所 suǒ (A) 'which'

對(他們)來說 duì (tāmen) lai shuō (PH) 'come to speak regarding (them)' — as far as (they) are concerned

新奇 xīnqí (SV) novel

親切 qīnqiè (SV) close and dear, familiar

留學 liúxué (V) study abroad

  留 liú (V) remain

提高 tígāo (V) raise, heighten, improve

了解 liǎojiě (V) understand

下 xià (M) a 'go' (verbal measure)

風土人情 fēngtǔ rénqíng (set phrase) local conditions (human and environmental)

實際 shíjì (SV/A) real(ly), actual(ly), concrete(ly)

體驗 tǐyàn (V) experience for oneself

億 yì (NU) hundred million

日常 rìcháng (SV) everyday, routine

難忘 nán-wàng (SV) memorable

上課 shàng kè (VO) give a lesson

鐵路 tiělù (N) railway

房屋 fángwū (collective N) houses, buildings

終於 zhōngyú (A) finally, at last

站臺 zhàntái (N) railway platform

攔住 lánzhù (V) stop, bar the way

代表 dàibiǎo (V) represent (CV) on behalf of (N) representative

不敢當 bù gǎn dāng (IE) unworthy of the honour; be flattered; would not presume

接 jiē (V) meet (on arrival)

興奮 xīngfèn (SV) excited

涼快 liángkuai (SV) pleasantly cool

汗 hàn (N) sweat

  一身汗 yì shēn hàn (NU M N) sweating all over

秋高氣爽 qiū-gāo qì-shuǎng (set phrase) autumn (sky) high and air bracing — clear and refreshing autumn weather

信 xìn (V) believe

香港 Xiānggǎng (PW) Hong Kong

護照 hùzhào (N) passport

錢包 qiánbāo (N) purse, wallet

叫 jiào (CV) by (in passive constructions)

偷　tōu (V) steal

走　-zou (V comp) away

廁所　cèsuǒ (N) lavatory

上廁所　shàng cèsuǒ (VO) go to lavatory

結果　jiéguǒ (N) result, outcome (MA) as a result, consequently

誤　wù (V) miss (train, bus, etc.)

班　bān (M) for scheduled journeys by public transport

真是! zhēnshi!(I) well really! the idea! bad show!

行李　xíngli (N) luggage

託運　tuōyùn (V) book/check through (baggage)

全　quán (A) entirely, completely (=完全) (SV) complete, whole, entire

手提包　shǒutíbāo (N) (hand)bag, hold-all

箱子　xiāngzi (N) suitcase, trunk, box

冬天　dōngtiān (TW) winter

衣服　yīfu (N) clothing, clothes

到時候　dào shíhou (PH) when the time comes

打字機　dǎzìjī (N) typewriter

口香糖　kǒuxiāngtáng (N) chewing gum

衛生紙　wèishēngzhǐ (N) toilet paper

衛生　wèishēng (N) hygiene (SV) hygienic

紙　zhǐ (N) paper

得了　déle (IE) that's enough, pack it in

說　shuō (V) reprove, criticize

打　dá (M) dozen

頓　dùn (M) measure for beating

動　dòng (V) move, touch

雙數　shuāngshù (N) even number

單數　dānshù (N) odd number

照片　zhàopiàn (N) photograph

頤和園　Yíhéyuán (PW) Summer Palace (outside Peking)

座　zuò (M) for bridges, mountains, etc.

橋　qiáo (N) bridge

十七孔橋　Shíqī kǒng Qiáo (PR) Seventeen Arch (lit: aperture) Bridge

借用　jièyòng (V) borrow for use, turn to some purpose, take up

一課書　yí kè shū (NU M N) a written lesson

隔開　gékāi (V) separate

連　lián (V) join, connect

PRESENTATION

天亮了!列車奔過了黑夜,也奔過了黃河!從車窗望出去,南方的青山綠水已經看不見了,眼前是一望無際的華北平原.藍色的天空像被水洗過一樣的明淨,昨晚的悶熱也讓涼爽的秋風吹得無影無蹤.那幾個要到北京語言學院去學習的英國學生昨天一天忙着跟同車的旅客談天兒,夜裏又沒睡好,清早被車上的廣播叫醒以後本來還想再睡一會兒,但是一看窗外,立刻就讓這開闊的景色吸引住了.愛照相的更是拿出照相機不停地尋找鏡頭,地裏的農作物,路上的騾馬大車,正在勞動的公社社員都被他們照下來了.這幾個年輕人已經在倫敦大學念過了一年中文,現在所看到的對他們來說是那麼新奇,又是那麼親切.他們來留學,一方面是要提高自己的漢語水平,一方面也是想了解一下中國各地的風土人情,實際體驗一下十億人的日常生活.火車上這三十多小時已經給他們上了難忘的一課.

列車漸漸地慢下來了,鐵路兩旁的房屋越來越多,終於北京站到了.這幾個英國同學剛下車站臺那邊兒就走過來一位戴眼鏡兒的中年人,把他們攔住了:

DIALOGUE

王: 你們幾位是英國來的同學吧?我姓王,代表北京語言學院來歡迎你們!

李: 真不敢當!王老師,您好!謝謝您來接我們.

王: 不客氣!你們大家好!怎麼樣,坐了兩夜一天的火車,夠累了吧?

李: 我們也許是太興奮了,一點兒也不覺得累.北京天氣真好,比南方涼快多了.前天在廣州從早到晚都是一身汗,腦子都給熱糊塗了.

176

王：北京已經熱過了，現在正是秋高氣爽的好時候。欸，你們一共不是九個人嗎？還有兩位呢？

李：說出來您也許不信，我們那兩個同學，一個在香港坐公共汽車，護照、錢包都叫人給偷走了，現在還在找呢；另外一個在廣州車站，開車以前跑去上廁所，結果誤了這班車。

王：欸！真是！希望他們明後天能到，等會兒我再跟廣州聯繫一下兒，你們行李都拿下來了嗎？有託運的沒有？

李：我們六個人的行李全都在這兒。白海倫除了這三個大手提包以外，還有幾件託運的。

王：你們六個人都是一個小箱子啊？冬天的衣服帶了嗎？

李：我們想實際體驗一下兒中國的生活，決定衣食住行都要跟中國同學一樣，沒有的東西到時候再買，所以行李很少。

王：那太好了！白同學有幾件託運的行李啊？

白：我⋯⋯

李：她大概不好意思說，一共六大件，您沒想到吧！從自行車到打字機；從口香糖到衛生紙，要甚麼有甚麼！

白：得了，得了，小李，我帶甚麼用不著你替我廣播，你先讓王老師看看你的箱子再說別人吧！

李：我就這麼一個小箱子，有甚麼好看的？

白：外頭是沒甚麼好看，可是裏頭呢？整整兩打咖啡！你要體驗中國生活帶咖啡來幹麼？

李：我⋯⋯我每天早晨不喝咖啡醒不了，要是醒不了，怎麼能去體驗生活呢？！

(1) A: 雪華，雪華，你來一下兒好嗎？

　　B: 甚麼事啊？我正在炒菜呢！這回又是甚麼東西找不着了？

　　A: 你看見我那張地圖沒有？本來放在桌子上，不知道叫誰給拿走了？

　　B: 昨天晚上你跟老黃看着地圖談旅行，是不是讓他借去了？

　　A: 沒有，沒有，老黃地圖多得很，我那張就是他送的。

　　B: 會不會叫小明拿去玩兒了？你問問他。

　　A: 這孩子上次玩兒我的小計算機，不是叫我好好兒地打了一頓嗎？我想他不敢再動我的東西了吧，你再幫我想想。

　　B: 你看風這麼大，窗戶又沒關，也許讓風給吹跑了。

　　A: 桌子上那麼多紙都沒吹走，地圖更吹不走了。

　　B: 你早上沒帶到學校去嗎？

　　A: 噢！學校？對了！我想起來了，我已經把地圖掛在辦公室的牆上了。真是這天氣！我都給熱糊塗了！

　　B: 你的腦子哪天清楚啊？！

(2) A: 時間過得真快，沒想到我們已經學了半年的中文了。

　　B: 是啊！這本書馬上就要學完了。

　　A: 你覺得這本書怎麼樣？

　　B: 我覺得相當不錯，不過有一點我不明白：為甚麼不多不少十七課？

　　A: 十七課不行嗎？

　　B: 行當然行，不過平常不是十六、十八就是二十、二十四，都是雙數，很少有單數的。

　　A: 本來我也奇怪這件事，後來看到一張頤和園的照片才明白。

　　B: 頤和園？這本書跟頤和園有甚麼關係？

　　A: 你忘了：頤和園不是有一座很漂亮的橋嗎？

　　B: 你是說那座聞名世界的十七孔橋？

　　A: 對了！就是十七孔橋！寫這本書的人大概是借用這個意思，希望這十七課書能像一座橋一樣，把被語言隔開的外國人民和中國人民連在一起！

178

SPEECH PATTERNS

(1) Passive constructions

(a) Passive in English, not in Chinese

1. 電報收到了,信還沒收到呢.
2. 我的護照已經拿到了,別的手續正在辦呢.
3. 在中國留學一年,他的漢語水平大大地提高了.
4. 汽車洗過了以後,看起來跟新的一樣.
5. 今天的糖醋魚真不錯,你看,連魚頭都吃了.
6. 行李送來了嗎? 箱子已經送來了,手提包還沒呢.
7. 這條新聞已經廣播到全世界了.
8. 秋天的晚上她常常站在海邊兒,吹着海風,想着以前的事.
9. 老王的自行車已經找到了. (是誰找到的? 不知道.)
   cf. 老王已經找到他的自行車了.
10. 東西都搬走了嗎? cf. 他們都搬走了嗎?

(b) With coverbs of agent 'bèi', 'jiào', 'ràng' and 'gěi'

Patterns:

a. receiver **bèi** V
   小 王 被 打 了.

b. receiver CVs of agent doer (**gěi**) V
   小 王 被/叫/讓 人 (給) 打 了.

c. receiver **gěi** doer V
   小 王 給 人 打 了.

1. 他們都被請去了.
2. 我們都被留在那兒了.
3. 他已經被拉上來了.
4. 他被問得說不出話來了.
5. 我們被關在一間黑屋子裏,連廁所都不准上.
6. 你的照相機能不能借我用一天? 對不起,已經被人借走了.
7. 我昨天買的口香糖呢? 都叫孩子給吃了.
8. 你的行李呢? 找不着了,大概被人拿錯了.

179

9. 我一下車就被兩個外國人攔住了.

10. 他們一家人坐在那兒,全叫電視給吸引住了.

11. 我正要用的那張紙讓風給吹到樹上去了.

12. 這件事如果讓他知道了,一定會替你廣播出去.

13. 他的護照飛機票都叫人偷走了嗎?　　沒有,只有錢被偷了.

14. 快進去吧,外頭這麼冷,別讓風給吹病了.

15. 你這麼糊塗,恐怕給人賣了都不知道.

(2) <u>Three types of sentences compared</u>

(a) Simply tells what happened
(b) Says what someone/something did with someone/something
(c) Says what happened to someone/something

1a. 他喝了一杯茶就走了.
 b. 他把那杯茶喝了.
 c. 那杯茶叫他給喝了.

2a. 他一個人吃了一桌菜,真能吃!
 b. 他一個人把一桌菜都吃了.
 c. 一桌菜都讓他一個人給吃了.

3a. 他打了小明一頓.
 b. 小明不聽他的話,他把小明打了一頓.
 c. 小明被他打了一頓,心裏很不高興.

4a. 有人偷了他的照相機.
 b. 有人把他的照相機偷走了.
 c. 他的照相機叫人偷走了.

5a. 風吹得我很不舒服.
 b. 風把我吹得很不舒服.
 c. 我被風吹得很不舒服.

6a. 他愛人賣了他的自行車,買了一架照相機.
 b. 因為沒錢買菜,他愛人把他的自行車賣了.
 c. 他的自行車呢?　　他的自行車叫他愛人給賣了.

180

(3) Appearance and disappearance

1. 你看,那邊兒飛過來一個甚麼東西?
2. 我們那條路上搬走了一家美國人,搬來了兩家德國人.
3. 太白山上發現了很多兩千年以前的東西.
4. 我們公司最近走了不少人.
5. 昨天我聽說圖書館裏新到了五千本中文書.
6. 奇怪,我錢包裏怎麼少了五塊錢?
7. 我們正在說話,忽然樓上走下來一位穿藍衣服的女學生.
8. 快看!男廁所裏走出來一個女孩子.
   那不是女孩子,你別以為頭髮長的都是女的.

(4) Verbal measures

1. 你在中國坐過幾次火車?
2. 這兒的事已經跟他說了三回了,好像他還是不太了解.
3. 他累得不得了,很想去睡一覺.
4. 他只愛舒服不愛勞動,又讓他爸爸說了一頓.
5. 我問她找誰,她看了我一眼就走了.
6. 不知道為甚麼他忽然跑過來打了我三下兒.
7. 我想跟你了解一下兒這兒的風土人情.
8. 我們都應該體驗一下兒勞動人民的生活.
9. 他拿起琴來彈了幾下兒,好聽極了.
10. 我找不着我弟弟了,能不能麻煩您廣播一下兒,他名字叫……
11. 明天我不能去歡迎他們,請你代表一下兒行不行?
12. 衣食住行的問題都得好好兒地研究一下兒.

(5) 'YĪ' for 'whole'

1. 這一手提包的書都是他新買的。
2. 天氣這麼熱,一勞動就是一身汗.
3. 電話響了,快去替我接一下兒.我正在洗碗,一手的水.

4. 你看他一身的雪,真像個大雪人兒.
5. 一飛機的旅客都叫窗外的景色吸引住了.
6. 誰在這兒洗東西了?怎麼搞得一地都是水?
7. 一屋子的酒都叫他兒子給喝了.
8. 一車的照相機都叫人給偷了.

(6) 'Zai' for action deferred

1. 今天太晚了,明天再去辦吧! (cf. 今天沒辦好,明天還要再去辦.)
2. 這件事應該怎麼辦? 等他來了再說吧!
3. 我想買點兒衛生紙. 家裏有那麼多,用完了再買吧.
4. 我得去問問他. 他還在睡覺呢,等他醒了再問他吧.
5. 經不經過香港,你們研究一下兒再決定吧.
6. 我跟他們聯繫以後再打電話給你,好不好?
7. 你先代表我去車站接他,明天早晨我再到旅館去看他.
8. 你先把打字學會了,再去找工作就容易多了.

(7) 'Suǒ'

1. 你所看到的都是勞動人民的實際生活.
2. 我們所研究的問題跟電子計算機沒甚麼關係.
3. 我們所能辦到的只有這一點.
4. 他們所用的法子聽說是最特別的.
5. 我們大家所希望的就是能把中文學好.

(8) The measure modified

1a. 他一共帶了六大件行李,吃的,穿的,甚麼都有.
 b. 他一共帶了六件大行李和兩個小手提包.
2a. 這麼一小本書就要十鎊錢,我不買.
 b. 這本小書對我很有用.

3a. 他送給我們三大包米，夠我們吃一年.
 b. 車上有不少肉還有三包大米.　　　(大米＝白米)
4a. 做這個菜得用三大碗油.
 b. 做這個菜得用三碗大油.　　　(大油, 'lard')
5a. 一進門，左邊兒立着一長排書架.
 b. 左邊兒是一排很長的書架.

ABBREVIATIONS FOR GRAMMATICAL TERMS

		First appeared in lesson
A	adverb	1
AT	attributive	9
BF	bound form	1
C	conjunction	5
CLV	classificatory verb	2
CV	coverb	9
I	interjection	2
IE	idiomatic expression	1
K	marker	5
L	localizer	8
LC	literary Chinese	3
M	measure	4
MA	movable adverb	4
MV	modal verb	3
N	noun	1
NU	number	3
O	object	3
P	particle	1
PH	phrase	9
PN	pronoun	1
PR	proper noun	9
PW	place word	2
QW	question word	2
S	subject	1
SP	specifier	2
SV	stative verb	1
TW	time word	1
V	verb	3
V-O	verb-object construction	3

VOCABULARY

Figures with entries refer to lesson numbers

a 啊 — 1	bàn shì 辦事 — 9	bì 幣 — 6
ài 愛 — 2,3	bànshìchù 辦事處 — 16	bì 必 — 10
àiren 愛人 — 2	bāng 幫 — 16	bìděi 必得 — 10
ān 安 — 9	bāng-máng 幫忙 — 16	bì 畢 — 11
	bàng 鎊 — 16	bì-yè 畢業 — 11
	bāo 包 — 5	biān(r) 邊(兒) — 8
	bǎo 飽 — 7	biàn 便 — 10
bā 八 — 4	bào 報 — 5	biǎo 錶 — 12
bǎ 把 — 15	bàogào 報告 — 16	biǎo 表 — 17
bà 爸 — 11	bēi 杯 — 4	bié 別 (SP) — 7
bàba 爸爸 — 11	bēizi 杯子 — 13	(A) — 9
ba 吧 — 2	běi 北 — 2,8	biéde (SP) 別的 — 7
bái 白 — 13	běibian(r) 北邊(兒) — 8	biéren 別人 — 12
báicài 白菜 — 15	běifāng rén 北方人 — 12	bìng 病 — 16
báicài niúròu tāng	Běihǎi Gōngyuán	bìngle 病了 — 16
白菜牛肉湯 — 15	北海公園 — 12	bō 播 — 17
báiqiējī 白切雞 — 15	Běijīng 北京 — 2	bù/bú 不 — 1
bǎi 百 — 9	Běijīng Yǔyán Xuéyuàn	búbì 不必 — 10
bǎihuò shāngdiàn	北京語言學院 — 17	bú-cuò 不錯 — 9
百貨商店 — 9	bèi 被 — 17	bú dàng yì huí shì
bǎi 擺 — 16	bēn 奔 — 17	不當一回事 — 15
bān 班 (N) — 12	běn 本 (M) — 4	búguò 不過 — 12
(M) — 17	(SP) — 14	bú (yào) kèqi
bān 搬 — 14	běnlái 本來 — 7	不(要)客氣 — 14
bāndào 搬到 — 14	bèn 笨 — 13	búlùn 不論 — 15
bàn 半 — 5	bǐ 筆 (N) — 5	bùdéliǎo 不得了 — 13
bàn 辦 — 9	(M) — 14	bùgǎndāng 不敢當 — 17
bànfǎ 辦法 — 12	bǐ 比 — 13	bù-hǎoyìsi
bàn-gōng 辦公 — 16	bǐfang 比方 — 13	不好意思 — 14
bàngōngshì 辦公室 — 16	bǐfang shuō 比方說 — 13	bù shūfu 不舒服 — 10
bàngōngzhuō 辦公桌 — 16	bǐjiào 比較 — 13	bùtíng(de) 不停(地) — 17

190

192